TAKE HEART

The Boston College Church in the 21st Century Series

Patricia De Leeuw and James F. Keenan, S.J.,
General Editors

Titles in this series include:

Handing On the Faith: The Church's Mission and Challenge

Sexuality and the U.S. Catholic Church: Crisis and Renewal

Priests for the 21st Century

Inculturation and the Church in North America

The Church in the 21st Century Center at Boston College seeks to be a catalyst and resource for the renewal of the Catholic Church in the United States by engaging critical issues facing the Catholic community. Drawing from both the Boston College community and others, its activities currently are focused on four challenges: handing on and sharing the Catholic faith, especially with younger Catholics; fostering relationships built on mutual trust and support among lay men and women, vowed religious, deacons, priests, and bishops; developing an approach to sexuality mindful of human experience and reflective of Catholic tradition; and advancing contemporary reflection on the Catholic intellectual tradition.

TAKE HEART

Catholic Writers on Hope in Our Time

edited by
BEN BIRNBAUM

A Crossroad Book
The Crossroad Publishing Company
New York

Excerpt from "Disgraceland," *Sinners Welcome: Poems by Mary Karr,* Copyright © 2006 by Mary Karr. Reprinted by permission of HarperCollins publishers.

Excerpt from Charles Péguy, *The Portal of the Mystery of Hope,* English translation of the 1986 critical edition (Grand Rapids: Wm. B. Eerdmans Publishing Co., 1996), reprinted by permission of the publisher.

The Crossroad Publishing Company
16 Penn Plaza – 481 Eighth Avenue, Suite 1550
New York, NY 10001

Copyright © 2007 by the Trustees of Boston College, acting by and through The Church in the 21st Century

All rights reserved. No part of this book may be reproduced, stored in a retrieval system, or transmitted, in any form or by any means, electronic, mechanical, photocopying, recording, or otherwise, without the written permission of The Crossroad Publishing Company.

Printed in the United States of America on acid-free paper

The text of this book is set in 11/16 Meridien.
The display face is Zapf Chancery.

Library of Congress Cataloging-in-Publication Data
Taking heart : Catholic writers on hope in our time / edited by
Ben Birnbaum.
     p. cm. – (The church in the 21st century series ; 5)
  ISBN-13: 978-0-8245-2461-6
  ISBN-10: 0-8245-2461-6 (alk. paper)
  1. Hope – Religious aspects – Catholic Church.
 I. Birnbaum, Ben. II. Title.
BV4638.T35 2007
234'.25 – dc22
                                 2007022596

1   2   3   4   5   6   7   8   9   10   12   11   10   09   08   07

Contents

Part Two
LOVE

Part Three
BELIEVE

Contents

Part Four
OTHER VOICES

Introduction

Scatter the Darkness

If a book can be said to have a genesis, this one traces back to the evening of September 30, 2002, when 350 or so men and women gathered for a public talk at Boston College, cramming themselves into a tiered classroom with a capacity of just under 300, the overflow sitting in the aisles and on the floor below the lectern and standing in a walkway high up at the back of the room, peering down "like gatecrashers behind Section 16 in Fenway Park," I reported at the time in *Boston College Magazine*.

Crowds for public lectures are certainly not unknown at Boston College, and over the years I have seen galleries jammed for the likes of Alan Bloom, Seamus Heaney, Cornel West, Noam Chomsky, and Ann Coulter.

Those crowds, however, were anomalous, their members lured away from the soft glow of television or cabernet by the blaze of celebrity, a coruscation that rarely radiates from the foreheads of those experts on Nigeria's delta, or the Dow's prospects, or Melville's soul who barnstorm the academic circuit with their well-reviewed books in hand, attracting crowds that could be conveyed home in half-a-dozen taxis at the conclusion of the coffee and tea reception in the corridor.

For the past twenty-five years or so, I have had a hand in trying to build these "crowds," and I know, therefore, that, generally speaking, a memoirist draws better than a journalist, who draws better than a novelist, who draws better than a poet, who draws better than an economist, who draws better than a theologian, unless the subject is sex, in which case the draw will always be respectable, even if a theologian is doing the talking. And this is why the evening of September 30, 2002, was remarkable from the outset, because the advertised draw was not one but *four* (count 'em) theologians, and serious ones (there are other kinds), the authors of such shelf-bowers as *The Legacy of the Tübingen School, New Commentary on the Code of Canon Law,* and *Motion and Motion's God: Thematic Variations in Aristotle, Cicero, Newton, and Hegel.* Moreover, their advertised topic was "Laity and the Governance of the Church: Legitimate Expectations," a title that seemed to promise — particularly given that "legitimate" speed bump — far more brake than throttle, and no sex at all.

Only a year earlier, a score of people might have gathered for such an occasion, and few of them would have been under the age of fifty, I'm guessing, or un-versed in Rahner, Aquinas, and the checkered history of proportionalism, for starters. But September 2002 was different because in January of that year the *Boston Globe* published, on its front page, a story about a defrocked dour-looking priest named John J. Geoghan under the headline "Church allowed abuse by priest for years," and by the time September 30 came around, several hundred sexual abuse lawsuits against the Boston archdiocese had been joined; Geoghan's victims (150 claimants came forward) had been offered $10 million in settlement; Cardinal Bernard Law had several times been deposed in court (he would resign his post in December); a prominent Boston businessman and philanthropist, Jack Connors Jr., had publicly recommended that lay Catholics temporarily withhold donations to the archdiocese and instead follow his lead in writing their checks to their own parishes and to charities; and William P. Leahy, S.J., the president of Boston College, had launched "The Church in the 21st Century," a project to bring the means of the university to bear upon what was almost invariably referred to as "the sexual abuse crisis" and to help locate means of understanding, remedy, and renewal.

On this September evening, the four theologians and their overflow audience had, in fact, been brought together under the aegis of the Church in the 21st Century, and the particular neuralgia set out for probing was the broken trust among lay Catholics, priests, and bishops, a pain that had come to predominate over the previous nine months, with new evidence tumbling out by the day, it sometimes seemed, indicating that Boston's archbishop and bishops had been aware of the criminal behavior of particular priests and in many cases complicit in the transfer of these men from parishes in which they were known to have committed rape to parishes in which they were not known.

Five years on, I must admit that I've forgotten the substance of the evening's talks, by which I mean the particular recommendations and cautions the panelists advanced to guide the audience in the repair of their church, diocese, parishes, and spirits. Preserved program notes and memory tell me that the four talks covered life in the early church, fractiousness in the nineteenth-century church, the purpose and scope of canon law, and the Second Vatican Council. I also know from my written notes that the *Life of St. Polycarp* came up, as did Cardinal Newman, the First Council of Nicea's fifteenth canon, which forbade diocese-jumping by ambitious or bored bishops and deacons, and *Lumen Gentium,* the Vatican II document that placed "the people of God" in common Catholic parlance. Also referenced was a joke by Ammianus Marcellinus, a prominent pagan chronicler of Rome's decline, which allowed one of the speakers to remark that those present had given Marcellinus his first laugh in sixteen centuries.

And I remember, most powerfully, the audience: men and women mostly of middle age and more, who received the speakers warmly, laughed easily, and stayed alert in their places for an hour and ten minutes, many of them scribbling, scribbling, scribbling on legal pads and in notebooks, like students in the week before the final exam, worried but sure of the possibilities, taut with hope.

Just how they happened to find or retain that hope in a time dizzy with betrayal, anger, and uncertainty is the question addressed by this book — a book, I should note, that contains no reports by anthropologists, geneticists, linguists, or psychiatrists on how hope may come to make a particularly knotty tangle in the culture or cells or vernacular or psyche of individuals who have been infused with Catholic Christianity. And readers hungering for this kind of knowledge are advised to buy other books (as well as this one). Here, however, we have taken an oblique, rather than systematic, approach to the question, asking serious and able Catholic writers, who may be expert at nothing more than serious and able writing, to "reflect on the nature of hope and its sources and uses in our time." It's an instruction both crisp and hazy, which, as we thought about it, seemed about right for writers, who are obliged to follow their pens anyway, and appropriate as well as a launching pad for considering hope — an entity that is as real as it is incredible (given what any adult knows about contingency).

A few of our respondents soon reported back that they could either not make our deadline or do the required work for the slight honorarium we offered (writing for small change is a sharp challenge to the hopes of those who write to put bread on the table), but only one replied that he could not join up because he was, on reflection, without hope. Two others eventually sent pieces disjointed and querulous enough to indicate that they, too, were out of something, maybe hope. For the vast majority of the individuals whom we initially queried, however, hope, if not instantly available, was close enough at hand, even "in our time."

The thirty-five contributions to this volume seem to me accessible enough that I shouldn't need to supply the program notes that are a convention of the editor's introduction: e.g., "and then there's Jones, who unlike Smith, but in absolute contrast with Brown, prefers paper to plastic." There are, however, four points I would like to make.

1. While our letter of invitation was clearly grounded in a consideration of the sexual abuse scandal, the essays here reflect not that disaster alone but the dizzying variety of woes that dampen human hope and at the same time call it up. "Nothing that is worth doing can be achieved in our lifetime; therefore we must be saved by hope," is Reinhold Niebuhr's well-known construction. My friend the Jesuit theologian James Keenan takes a more grounded (Catholic) approach. Hope, he has written, "is always somewhere near the cross or the empty tomb."

2. However, at the same time as they draw inspiration from the personal and particular, these thirty-five essays — thirty-two by Catholics and three by a control group comprising a rabbi, an Orthodox priest, and

a Lutheran minister — avoid (for the most part) treating hope in its narrow sense, a variety known as "intentional hope," by which is meant the hope (my hope, in fact) that Cherry Garcia ice cream will be found to moderate high blood pressure. Rather, the hope plumbed on these pages is of the "dispositional" sort, which is the hope that is always there, as present to human beings as is the Van Allen belt to the world, or more pertinently for this book, as present as is God to Catholic believers. As resonances go, dispositional hope is merely a hope; it cannot drown out the roar of what happens. But it is sturdy enough to be heard and tracked by those who have learned to listen for it and attend to it.

The French Catholic philosopher Gabriel Marcel, a man as good on hope as any being who walked the planet during the late, disastrous century, points in this direction when he describes dispositional hope as "active patience." He writes in *The Philosophy of Existentialism:* "Hope consists in *asserting* [emphasis added] that there is at the heart of being, beyond all data, beyond all inventories and all calculations, a mysterious principle which is in connivance with me" — a "mysterious principle" that contributors to this book would see as the Source of hope.

3. However they are attuned to, and yearn for, this ultimacy, our contributors have ears, tongues, fingers, and bellies and associate their hopes with a wide range of *things,* including green chile, a blooded crossroad, a

Monday evening meditation group, a subway ride, charm bracelets, "Danny Boy," a neglected church building, an AIDS clinic, and Spanish anarchists. This is a book, in fact, packed with *things,* and attention is paid to them, as is appropriate in a collective work made by men and women for whom all begins with a first sentence that includes "and the spirit of God hovered over the face of the waters," and a first chapter that seven times, and on sound authority, declares the created world "good."

4. The editor of this book, largely made by and for Catholics, is not a Catholic, and he undertook and began this project without knowledge of what was said about hope by the Baltimore Catechism ("Hope is the virtue by which we firmly trust that God, who is all-powerful and faithful to His promises, will in His mercy give us eternal happiness and the means to obtain it"), or Aquinas (hope has a twofold object), or Jim Keenan, or for that matter any theologian who contributed to one or more of the 121 books in the Boston College library whose titles turn up when one teases the search engine with the Library of Congress formula "Christianity – Aspects – Hope." Moreover, I began this project without having thought deeply about hope as a theological business, for Judaism, the tea in which I've long steeped, doesn't make much of a fuss about hope at all (faith and charity are another matter, and particularly charity). This is not to say that hope is of no consequence in Judaism, but only that it is an inherence rather than an efflorescence, acknowledged

rather than celebrated. (A Boston College library search undertaken with "Judaism" in place of "Christianity" in the string yields two records, and one is a book jointly authored by Elie Wiesel and the German Catholic theologian Johann Baptist Metz. Oy.) At the bottom of this is, I imagine, a Jewish set of eschatological expectations that is more tempered than those that pleasure and entangle Christians. In fact, my favorite manifestation of the Jewish view of hope is a maxim with an eschatological tang that is found in a late book of the Talmud and attributed (improbably) to the great first-century rabbi Yochanan ben Zakai: "If you have a sapling in your hand, and someone says to you that the Messiah has come, stay and complete the planting, and then go to greet the Messiah."

The editor being who he is and pretty much formed at this point, this book is not — and could never have been — a teaching. It was driven by no special knowledge or plan except the usual editorial scheme, which is to try to learn something you don't know by collecting a set of human voices in a book and seeing what sound comes off the pages. "There can be no hope," Marcel writes, "that does not constitute itself through a we and for a we. I would be tempted to say that all hope is at the bottom choral."

Though the chorus metaphor is appealing, and though Marcel is to my mind right (a thorough Catholic who hopes while adrift alone on an ice floe in the Bering Sea would, it seems to me, be of necessity hoping in communion), what we have here is not quite a choral work. In fact, the internal dissonances are manifold and unambiguous, and it's clear that a number of tunes are being sung and that a number of our contributors who would think nothing of sharing space (and silence) at the communion rail would be requesting seat changes within an hour if placed in similar proximity on a longish airplane flight. But then we're talking about a catholic people as well as a Catholic communion, the "here comes everybody" church, to use a tagline that's often applied these days — borrowed from one of the more anomalous geniuses nurtured in the church's ample bosom. In the end, when it came time to analyze the parts that made up the score, I did discover that in spite of their differences, each person who contributed to this book (and I include members of the control group) wanted to Build, Love, or Believe in the face of the howling wind; and that, I hope, is enough to justify this book as a Catholic as well as catholic enterprise.

Finally, I offer thanks to my staff in Boston College's Office of Marketing Communications, and particularly to my co-conspirator and fellow Brooklynite William Bole. Each time I use the editorial "we" in this introduction, it is an arm flung around Bill's sturdy shoulders. I thank, as well, Betsy Brandes, who developed the cover design, and all other of my colleagues who felt the edge of my irritability each time this project approached a deadline and

I was compelled to mutter that a man with a full-time job ought never accept the responsibility to develop a book with thirty-five contributors unless he's been offered a sabbatical at the same time. Finally, my appreciation to the former president of Boston College J. Donald Monan, S.J., and the university's current president, William P. Leahy, S.J., who, for reasons not clear to everyone at all times, have for decades allowed me to get away with doing work that made sense to me. This book is small thanks for that liberty.

Ben Birnbaum
Chestnut Hill, Massachusetts

Part One

BUILD

∾ 1 ∾

Hope against Hope
Paul J. Griffiths

Hope's anticipatory delight is always woven together with the melancholy of absence and the tension of uncertainty. What you hope for is something you think you'd like that isn't present (if it were you wouldn't be hoping for it), which explains the melancholy; and it's something you may not get (if you were certain you'd get it you wouldn't be hoping for it), which explains the tension. And these are just the surface difficulties connected with hope. Much deeper is the realization, shared, I should think, by just about everyone over the age of thirty, that even when you do get what you hope for, you generally find it disappointing. The pleasure to be had in hope generally exceeds the pleasure gained from getting what you hoped for, and this in turn means that hope itself may not be something to be hoped for. For if the likely upshot of any particular hope is one of two disappointments — that produced by not getting what you hope for, and the other by getting it only to find

15

that it's less than you anticipated — then why hope for hope?

The remedy for this hopeless situation is, fortunately, clear. It is to hope for the right things: things, that is, that are likely to happen, thus reducing the possibility of the first disappointment; and things that, once gotten, will be all you hoped they'd be, or more, thus removing the possibility of the second disappointment. Some parts of this optimistic hope-pruning program can be carried out without too much difficulty. I can learn fairly easily not to hope for impossibles, such as having met St. Augustine; and I can with only a little more difficulty reduce my tendency to hope for the very unlikely, such as world peace before I die or the abolition of cellphones and email by divine fiat. But I do much less well, as I expect we all do, in ceasing to hope for things that won't disappoint me should I get them. So although the remedy for hope's double melancholy is clear enough in principle, it proves difficult to put into practice unless you're willing to take the deeply ascetical line of reducing your hopes to almost nothing.

I'm of a temperament that finds this ascetical line attractive. But I'm also a Catholic, and the Catholic tradition has no time for ascetical stoicism. Most human beings, Catholic or not, don't either. Most of us seem quite prepared to put up with hope's inevitable disappointments. We are, naturally, what Catholicism would want us to be, which is meta-hopers, hopers against hope. What other tradition has, or would want, a patron saint of lost causes, which is to say of hopeless cases? Hope is woven deeply into the fabric of Catholic thought and life. It is, technically, a theological and infused virtue, which is to say a good habit given us (when we're lucky enough to have it) by unmerited gift of God, one that we could not develop ourselves, by our own effort — and it is so because its antonym, despair, is certainly a mortal sin, and, according to some, exactly the sin against the Holy Spirit that cannot be forgiven. It should be easy enough to see why: despair of a radical and systematic sort, the extinction of all hope, means that repentance is impossible, for repentance makes no sense without hope for the possibility of amendment. Sincere intention to amend your life requires the hope that this is possible, even against a crushing weight of evidence as to its unlikeliness. We must also pray, and thus hope for, such profoundly unlikely things as world peace, the salvation of all people, and the conformity of the world to Christ. I judge these things to be profoundly unlikely to happen short of the second coming, but I must nonetheless hope for them.

This means that I have an important place for lament in my life. The necessity of hope against hope — for the purification of the church I love; for the shedding of less innocent blood; for a replacement of hatred, suspicion, and fear by love, openness, and confidence; for the progressive removal of my own compulsive sins and disorders — brings lament with it, the rending of at least my heart if not my garments. These two, hope and lament, cannot be separated in a fallen world, and my own sense of what it means to be a Catholic encourages me in the thought that it would be a mistake to attempt their separation. To hope in a single-mindedly optimistic way would be absurd and superficial; to lament without hope would be, strictly, damnable. And so the intertwining of hope and lament will I expect (but do not hope) to stay with me until hope falls finally and irreversibly away. This will happen should I enter that place in which all hope is abandoned forever; it will also happen, but differently, should I enter that place in which there is no need for hope because I shall know as I am known. For the second of these I hope, for myself as for all. But I do not do so with confidence.

> *Even when you do get what you hope for, you generally find it disappointing.*

And as for shorter-term hopes, hopes for a reform of the church (*ecclesia semper reformanda*, it should always be remembered), for wisdom in high places, for a recall of the dogs of war, for food for the hungry, water for the thirsty, comfort for the lonely — these I have, but they are preceded by lament that hopes for such things are necessary at all, and followed by lament that they will not be fully realized. It is a dark time we live in, as it always has been and always, until the eschaton, will be. I try not to let hope for these things be overwhelmed by lament and thus edge toward despair, but it is difficult. Perhaps it should be difficult: we must, after all, act in support of peace, justice, and love while knowing that what we do will not bring these hopes to fruition. But sometimes, as now, the darkness of the times becomes oppressively visible, almost tangible, and I cannot press my way through it. The days and nights flicker past as rapidly as a weaver's shuttle, and each seems to move the world deeper into blood and suffering and death: hope recedes into the unimaginable future. I take comfort then from Job, who cursed his birth and lamented his suffering but did not despair; from Abraham, who bound Isaac without despairing of God's promises; and, more than all, from Jesus, who lamented on the cross without despair, and whose willing embrace of suffering and death gave the world the only hope it has.

∾ 2 ∾

Practice

Lisa Sowle Cahill

Gaudium et Spes, one of the best-known documents of Vatican II, begins, "The joys and hopes, the griefs and anxieties, of the men of this age, especially those who are poor or in any way afflicted, these too are the joys and hopes, the griefs and anxieties, of the followers of Christ." The title of *Gaudium et Spes* is derived from its frequently quoted first phrase: "joys and hopes." Yet the follow-up phrase, "griefs and anxieties," might seem better suited to the "followers of Christ" today.

To many, the Catholic Church has betrayed the hopes generated by the council itself for church renewal and prophetic leadership in a world beset by wars and violence, poverty and racism, and discrimination against women in church and society. (Though *Gaudium et Spes,* written in 1965, employs male-oriented language, it notes approvingly that, in modern times, "women claim an equity with men before the law and in fact" [no. 9].)

20

Catholics in the United States may observe with chagrin that the church has had scant success in bringing our society in line with episcopal and papal condemnations of the war in Iraq, exhortations to economic solidarity and restraint of market capitalism, and demands that all life be respected, whether of unborn children, poor women and families, the ill and elderly, racial and ethnic "minorities," or recent immigrants. U.S. Catholics are still reeling from a sex abuse crisis that revealed systemic perversions of the church's authority structure, disrespect for the voices and needs of laity, particularly children, and incredible hypocrisy regarding sexual morality and responsibility. Catholic "followers of Christ" may be tempted to despair that their church can effectively voice and represent the millions who are "poor or in any way afflicted," and may even feel that griefs, anxieties, and afflictions are being perpetrated by the church against its own members.

Yet hope gains a foothold in the daily lives and struggles of Catholics in the United States and around the world who take practical steps to improve the lives of those around them, nourish awareness of God's presence, and serve the common good. Hope is a practical virtue. Hope is not blind trust that "everything will work out" despite all evidence to the contrary. Hope is no mere expectation of an "eternal reward" despite the burdens and disappointments of life in the present. Neither does hope depend on or require some global assurance that on balance the world is becoming a better place, or that the church is making steady progress toward the reign of God that Jesus proclaimed to be "at hand" more than two thousand years ago (Mark 1:14). Hope takes root in the human heart when we commit to make a difference for the good, and when we join with others to do our part. Even limited, local successes increase our confidence, energize our efforts, and enlarge our hope. Hope is not just an emotion or a mental state; it is a virtue that must be cultivated by active resistance to difficulty and by positive action for change.

When asked about the challenge of keeping hope alive when working with people in extreme situations of poverty or violence, the liberation theologian Gustavo Gutiérrez replied, "Hope is giving some security for the possibility of change," through ordinary parish and community activities that fight injustice and human suffering. "It is therefore important to engage people into processes of dialogue that help them realize their capacity to change the situation of suffering on the ground and create a new hope for themselves."

In the processes that realize hope, religious persons sense the presence of a transcendent power that sustains their endeavors, a presence that grows stronger as they themselves respond. Christians see hope, and the corresponding power for action, as gifts of the Holy Spirit and of Christ's transforming love in communities of faith. In the New Testament, the letter called 1 Peter, written near the end of the first century C.E. for a church that had undergone persecution, reminds followers of Christ that they must always be ready to make "an accounting for the hope that is in you" (1 Pet. 3:15). The author is clear that hope is best accounted for by a concrete way of life characterized by love, compassion, and generosity. "All of you have unity of spirit, sympathy, love for one another, a tender heart, and a humble mind. Do not repay evil for evil or abuse for abuse" (3:9). "Now who will harm you if you are eager to do what is good? . . . Do not fear what they fear and do not be intimidated" (3:13–14). Though the way of love, justice, and hope is arduous, God will "restore, support, strengthen, and establish you" (5:10). This way of life is more than individual relationships and good deeds. It is a work of community-building.

These truths were brought home to me at a conference on Catholic peace building networks that I attended in Bujumbura, Burundi, in July 2006. Sponsored by Catholic Relief Services and the University of Notre Dame, this event brought together theologians, bishops, parish and diocesan workers, and Catholic peace activists from the African Great Lakes region, including Rwanda, Burundi, the Democratic Republic of Congo, and Uganda. Their peoples have suffered tremendous war, ethnic violence and genocide, and poverty in recent decades. Some of their own clergy and bishops betrayed them by condoning and even participating in murderous conflicts among Tutsis and Hutus. And, as with the sex abuse scandal in the United States, representatives of the "official" church have been very slow to admit wrongdoing, publicly repent, and call the church to change. Yet, despite their pain and questioning, the Catholics convened in Bujumbura were strong in faith and hope. They challenged one another and shared experiences and strategies, "griefs and anxieties," and success stories. Despite failings and setbacks, they were actively engaged at every level, from Christian base communities to regional conferences of bishops, working to overcome the trauma of violence within church and local communities, and to fight for fair elections, equal protection under law, and human rights in their nations.

Did they have a guarantee that peace would soon come to their region, or that divisions in society and church would forever end? No. Yet these African Christians would literally not be able to survive without the kind of hope that is a practical, community-building virtue. They give an accounting for their hope by their actions. They also remind me, a North American academic, of the pitfalls of what Sharon Welch, author of *A Feminist Ethic of Risk,* has termed "the ideology of cultured despair." Cultured despair is marked by an "erudite awareness of the extent and complexity of many forms of injustice," a knowledge that causes paralysis "in the sense of being unable to act in defiance of that injustice." The antidote to cultured despair is creative action

24

that is expert in "the art of the possible," and heartened by possibilities that are limited but real.

Hope and possibility are alive and available in the U.S. church and in society if we creatively seek them out. My personal list would include the rewards of teaching theology at a first-class university with a strong Jesuit, Catholic heritage, a commitment to social justice, and a tradition of open and respectful intellectual and theological exchange; opportunities to work constructively with colleagues at different points on the Catholic ideological spectrum through the Church in the 21st Century project at Boston College; the discovery of a community of faith and friendship in my local parish, where we have weathered tough times and survived the wiser; and the gift, as a Christian and a scholar, to support the struggles of Catholics in less privileged parts of the globe, learning from them to cultivate hope as a practical virtue.

❦ 3 ❧

Thickening Agent

Gregory Wolfe

I find myself smack in the Dantean "midway" spot — in the thick of marriage, child-rearing, and career-building. And I look for hope in the expected places: the maturation and flourishing of my children, the gradual movement from chronic financial anxiety to a measure of security, small gestures of recognition from the world for the work I do.

On each of these fronts, hope often seems to be in short supply, not because I have suffered any catastrophes but because there's always something else to worry about.

Looking for hope in the wider world seems even more challenging. When talking about society or culture or church, when is the news ever good enough to support real, substantial hope?

One of the oddities of hope is that it is allegedly a virtue, and as such it is something one is supposed to practice, cultivate, nurture. Yet few of us know exactly what exercising this virtue might look like. More than faith and love, the other two theological virtues, hope seems to be something that suddenly irrupts into our lives — perhaps in those moments when, in spite of what we know, we let our breath out. As a poster that hung over my bed in college said, quoting Aristotle: "Hope is a waking dream."

And yet I feel as though I have had a fairly intense relationship with this least understood of virtues. In a fashion I cannot fully account for, hope has asserted itself in my life, like some primitive internal force, something closer to a survival instinct than the exercise of virtue.

Groomed in my youth to be a conservative culture warrior, whose stock in trade is the notion that the world is in irreversible decline, the only hope I and my comrades in arms harbored took the form of political victory. We sought a transfer of power.

Then, in the early 1980s, just as conservatism swept into power (and half my colleagues became government bureaucrats), I found myself deserting the cause, mustering out, walking away from victory. Politicization and ideology — pervasive on both sides of the aisle — had reduced the philosophical principles I had cherished to instruments of raw power, a culture of fear, and relentless negativism.

It occurred to me that politics became meaningless when culture failed to generate the meanings and manners that give shape and purpose to the political process. A hyper-politicized society dissolves in its own acids.

Before I fully understood what I was doing, I began to move in the direction of generation, of thickening the culture rather than thinning it out.

I began to focus on two of the primary thickening agents for culture: art and religious faith. The result was the founding of a literary quarterly, *Image,* which features art and literature that grapple with the Judeo-Christian tradition, seek to "make it new," to use Ezra Pound's motto for the mission of the artist.

The editorial in the first issue of *Image* said, in part: "A culture is governed by its reigning myths. In the latter days of the twentieth century, there is an increasing sense that materialism, whether of the Left or Right, cannot sustain or nourish our common life. Religion and art share the capacity to help us to renew our awareness of the ultimate questions: who we are, where we have come from, and where we are going. In their highest forms religion and art unite faith and reason, grace and nature; they preserve us from the twin errors of superstition and rationalist abstraction."

As comparative literature scholar Virgil Nemoianu puts it, art and culture provide the "tumbling ground" in which otherwise abstract principles meet the ambiguities and complexities of the world. In this sense, as some of its critics point out, art can be a subversive activity.

But there are varieties of subversion. One can be a subversive in the name of a higher truth. Art does this when it prevents truth and goodness from becoming harsh and moralistic.

As I began my own efforts to thicken the culture, I looked to history for inspiration. It was in the lives and writings of the Renaissance Christian humanists — particularly in those of Erasmus and his circle — that I found my role models. While the culture wars of their time raged, the Christian humanists celebrated the imagination — always believing that a culture informed by faith could synthesize and heal the conflicts of the time. They inspired popes as well as reformers.

That the Christian humanist vision was obscured by the onset of the Reformation and the century of religious war that followed is not a count against their witness to hope. The legacy they left us is one of the richest in our heritage. Erasmus and his friends bequeathed to us a host of tools by which to understand and address the world, including the disciplines of biblical criticism, philology, history, and literary criticism. They advocated the education of women and wrote impassioned pleas against persecution of the Jews. In masterpieces like More's *Utopia* and Erasmus's *The Praise of Folly,* these humanists demonstrated that irony, satire, and wit — the subversive weapons of the imagination — can be handmaidens to faith.

Of course, as I have had reason to remind myself many times, art is not a substitute for religion. Yet as I attempt to live out my faith, I have been attracted to those who believe in the importance of making doctrine incarnate in culture.

I find particular hope in the phenomenon of Catholic lay movements that have emerged in recent decades. While their charisms vary a great deal — and some may even be inspired by culture wars for which I personally have no stomach — it seems to me that the best of these movements are concerned with thickening the culture of faith and rebuilding Christian community. To be sure, these associations exist to catechize and inspire piety, but most of them do so through forms of cultural and social engagement.

The movement I follow, Communion and Liberation, was founded by an Italian priest, Luigi Giussani, half a century ago. At the heart of Fr. Giussani's charism is the simple belief that Christianity is first and foremost an event — the event of the Incarnation of Christ and the encounter we have with Christ in our daily lives. In short, faith is dramatic. To forget this is to fall into mere moralism and varieties of theological correctness. Perhaps unsurprisingly, Fr. Giussani leavened his writings with allusions to Dante, and T. S. Eliot, Charles Péguy and Fyodor Dostoevsky.

The hope I experience in the companionship of Communion and Liberation is not the thrill of belonging to some esoteric order. Like any charism in the church, Communion and Liberation has its own distinctive form. But the purpose of that form is to return one to the origin of the Christian experience — the dramatic encounter with the Event.

As Msgr. Lorenzo Albacete, one of the leaders of Communion and Liberation in North America, has put it: "Our task is not a cultural battle as such, even if others see it that way and struggle against us and we must resist. Our task is to build the church. The rest is in the Father's hands."

Where it belongs.

~ 4 ~

The Work

James Martin, S.J.

The widespread closing of parishes in Boston demoralized thousands of Catholics throughout New England. A Vatican directive restricting gay men from the priesthood demoralized many gay Catholics, and a lot of straight ones as well. The sex abuse crisis demoralized almost every Catholic in the United States. And the Vatican's removal of the editor of *America* magazine, where I work, demoralized me. Should I go on?

I don't think I have to. There aren't many people who would say that these are bright times in the Catholic Church, at least in the United States. Sometimes the bad news seems overwhelming: another priest accused of molesting young boys (or girls), another bishop revealed to have transferred an abusive priest from parish to parish, another prominent theologian silenced for his writings, another lay worker removed from her job for criticizing the church, and so on.

Are things really as hopeless as they seem?

32

In such moments, I always find it helpful to go back to the experience of the early church for inspiration. In the first few hours after the crucifixion, the disciples of Jesus were dejected over the death of their leader. They were also frightened. The Gospel of John portrays them as cowering behind locked doors (John 20:19).

Most likely, this story is firmly grounded in history. When contemporary Scripture scholars attempt to sort out what stories are based in fact and what might be later additions by the writers of the Gospels, one criterion they apply is that of "embarrassment." As John Meier points out in his monumental series on the historical Jesus, called *A Marginal Jew,* those actions or sayings of Jesus in the Gospels that would have "embarrassed or created difficulties" for the early church are probably historically accurate. In other words, the evangelists would hardly have gone out of their way to make things up that cast Jesus or the apostles in a bad light. So it seems clear that the disciples were plainly terrified after the crucifixion and unwilling to hope in something unforeseen.

Think about what this means. Despite their having been with Jesus and having seen his miraculous healings of the sick, witnessed his amazing command of the winds and the seas, and heard his hope-filled message about the coming of the kingdom of God, his death robbed them of hope. The men and women who had the least reason to fear — that is, those who knew Jesus personally and saw what he could do — grew hopeless.

So perhaps it's not surprising that those of us who have *not* seen Jesus in the flesh sometimes feel a loss of hope. Hopelessness has a long pedigree in the church.

The answer to the hopelessness of the disciples was the resurrection. And, to my mind, the best "proof" of the resurrection is that after their encounter with the Risen Christ the disciples went from cowering behind locked doors to boldly proclaiming their faith in Jesus, even at the risk of persecution and death. During my theology studies, I read one theologian who posited that the "real" resurrection consisted of the disciples sitting around a table remembering Jesus and his life. And I thought, *Baloney!* Nothing as bland as that could turn a group of people from fearful to fearless. Only something as dramatic and life-altering as seeing the Resurrected Christ could effect such a transformation.

During these dark days in the church, this is what affords me hope: the resurrection. And one message of the resurrection is that things are never as dark as they seem, that Christ can quickly upend our doleful expectations, and that God can make all things new. One sees countless examples of this throughout church history: St. Francis of Assisi appearing on the scene when the church needed him most; Dorothy Day stepping onto the stage when we needed someone to point us to the poor in an increasingly affluent world; and the Second Vatican Council ushering in new insights when many parts of the church required renewal. Just as the apostles should not have doubted the power of the Lord to conquer death, so we should not doubt the power of the Spirit to conquer our own hopelessness today.

Hopelessness and its cousin, despair, are dead ends in the spiritual life for individuals as well as institutions. In his classic manual on prayer, *The Spiritual Exercises,* St. Ignatius Loyola, the sixteenth-century mystic and founder of the Jesuit order, reminded us that it is characteristic of what he calls the "evil spirit" to lead people into despair, to "cause gnawing anxiety, to sadden and to set up obstacles." In this way, says St. Ignatius, we can be prevented from progressing in the spiritual life. Things are hopeless, we sometimes feel, and nothing can change. Eventually we stop hoping and give up.

Despair can also be understood as a subtle form of pride. As the Trappist monk Thomas Merton says in his book *New Seeds of Contemplation,* despair is the development of a pride so absolute that it refuses to accept the fact that God can change things. In other words, hopelessness says that I alone know what is going to happen, and that it will be bad. Of course there are some times when things do seem hopeless — during a terminal illness, the rupture of a relationship, or the loss of a job. One is naturally sad in these times. But despair goes further than sadness or grief. Despair denies that God can work through even the saddest of situations. This is what the first disciples may have been feeling in the wake of the crucifixion.

The antidote to despair is hope. In the Catholic tradition, hope is one of the three "theological virtues," along with faith and charity, which is bestowed on us by God. But this doesn't mean that hope doesn't require some effort on our part. Hope isn't something we fill ourselves up with — as if we were topping off our tanks at a gas station — and then simply draw from. The hope that God gives has to be nurtured. Hope takes work.

Part of this work involves actively looking for signs of hope and being grateful for them. During the sexual abuse crisis, one of the few glimmers of hope that I found was in the vociferous response of many among the Catholic laity, who loudly and rightly condemned not only the perpetrators of the sexual abuse crimes, but also those bishops who had reassigned them. In the Second Vatican Council's document *Lumen Gentium,* the council fathers wrote that the laity "have the right and are indeed sometimes duty-bound to express their opinions on matters concerning the good of the church." After the abuse crisis I thought: Well, here is the laity, doing just that. This gave me hope.

Prayer is also an important way to nurture hope. As a Jesuit, I use a form of prayer recommended by St. Ignatius, called the "examination of conscience." And the first part of that prayer is gratitude. You thank God for the good things in your day. Often this is when you become most aware of the gift of hope. A few weeks ago, for example, a close Jesuit friend died, a priest who could accurately be described as my "spiritual father." He had taught me how to pray, had directed several of my retreats, and had even counseled my family during difficult times. David died unexpectedly, at age sixty-five. The news of his death plunged me into a brief but intense state of hopelessness and even despair. Who would be around to support me? To accompany me? What would I do without my spiritual father?

His funeral, at a large church in Boston, was literally standing room only. David had been a parish priest before entering the Jesuits and spent most of his life as a spiritual director. As a result, the pews were packed with an astonishing variety of people: members of his large Irish-Catholic family; former parishioners of all ages; men and women from dozens of religious orders; as well as scores of his Jesuit brothers. As his coffin left the church, I looked back and saw the packed pews and realized the value of being a good priest who does a few things very well: he prays, he listens, and he loves the People of God. I saw, as if never before, the value of the priesthood. In the midst of my hopelessness, I was filled with hope.

I knew that this hope was from God, because — like the hope that the first disciples experienced on Easter Sunday — it was both unexpected and unlike anything I could have imagined. And I felt myself once again ready to go out and preach the good news, the good news of hope.

❧ 5 ❧

Only Build

Msgr. Lorenzo Albacete

It often seems that all we see is the evidence of T. S. Eliot's judgment in "Choruses from the Rock":

> And the Church does not seem to be wanted
> In country or in suburb; and in the town
> Only for important weddings.

The church today does seem to have become "The Stranger / The God-shaken / ..." However, that is not the ultimate truth about the church's presence in the world. There is something else. There is another judgment, another last word about the state of the church.

"The Church must be forever building, and always decaying, and always being restored," Eliot continues. The Church is always "decaying," and often this decay is what one first sees. However, together with this, there is also the "building," the restoration (through conversion giving birth to saints), which is also always happening. This continual restoration, which can also be verified as the evidence of Christ's victory present in the world, is the basis for our hope for the Church today. This is no different today than at any other time, and so will be until Christ's victory is fully manifested. The Church is "forever building, for it is forever decaying within and attacked from without."

To see this, to verify this, it is enough to look in our hearts.

We are true children of our time, subject to the same temptations as anyone else. Our response to these temptations, to these threats to faith that we face today, shapes the way the "building" of the church takes place as the manifestation of Christ's victory and therefore our victory, the victory of humanity.

We do not seek to live the life of another time, but to live and build the church in the time we have been given, in the place we have been given.

The question asked of us who claim to be followers of Jesus Christ today is this one: "Does our faith interpret adequately the characteristic experiences of postmodern men and women, and if so, how?" We really should not speak of facing a "crisis" of faith. Instead, we should be aware of having a task before us, a mission to accomplish.

This world, such as it is, has already been embraced by the event of Christ. He is *Lumen Gentium,* "Light of the Nations," for all peoples and in all times, including this one. His light is already present in this historical time, touching the freedom of the people of our time, calling that freedom to respond. No circumstance can prevent this. He has already overcome death, and "the very gates of hell" cannot prevail against him and the fruits of his work. This world is embraced by his victory, interwoven in a sublime way by grace and liberty. Our task is to recognize his presence, to live by it, to live the freedom and happiness to which it gives birth, and to be its witnesses to others. All else is in the hands of the Father.

We are not called to run away from any circumstance. We must not be afraid to live the circumstances of life passionately, squeezing from them the "hope that does not disappoint."

We are not blind to all the great present obstacles to this hope. Still, it is the grace and freedom of Christ present today that allows us to recognize and see the obstacles of this historical epoch. We recognize the cultural prevalence of a way of looking at reality that is the mortal enemy of our destiny. We are not idiots, sentimentalists, purveyors of illusion, or utopians. We can see all of this clearly, and it saddens us, but we are aware that if we can see this it is only because we have experienced something that allows us to see more, to recognize the Presence of something more.

The task before us today is to sustain the vision of this "more," this opening of the human horizon to infinity. Our task is to confirm the presence of the Mystery in spite of a way of looking at reality that excludes it.

The task before us is indeed great and tiring, and it involves painful contradictions, but we are confident that nothing can stand in the way of Christ's victory. The Way of the Cross is the way to Easter.

The real problem is not the absence of Christ's victory. Our failure is the failure to recognize the anthropological, social, and cosmic implication of this victory in all the circumstances of life today. This is our mission: to witness that the reasons for faith are the same reasons for living liberty and seeking the true satisfaction of the desires in our heart.

> *We must not be afraid to live the circumstances of life passionately, squeezing from them the "hope that does not disappoint."*

Our analysis of the present situation should not make us confuse the diagnosis with the therapy. It is not a matter of opposing what is wrong with what is right, even though we must always publicly proclaim the truth. Our task is not a "cultural battle" as such, even if others see it that way and struggle against us, and we must resist. Our task is to witness and propose the encounter with the living presence of a man who said, "I am the way, the truth, the life," and allowed himself to be killed because of his desire to make us happy.

This is how we build the Church. The rest is in the Father's hands. As Eliot tells us, this is what men and women really yearn for and what we desire to share with all as children of today:

> The river flows, the seasons turn,
> The sparrow and startling have no time to waste.
> If men do not build,
> How shall they live?
> When the field is tilled
> And the wheat is bread
> They shall not die in shortened bed
> And a narrow sheet. In this street
> There is no beginning, no movement, no peace and
>   no end
> But noise without speech, food without taste.
> Without delay, without haste
> We would build the beginning and the end of this
>   street.
> We build the meaning:
> A Church for all
> and a job for each
> Each man to his work.

6

Shatter

Brian Doyle

The most extraordinary moment of my Catholic life-time was when little Angelo Roncalli politely grabbed the church he loved by its ancient hoary throat and shook it until the dust fell like snow.

But that was forty years ago, and that twenty-third John died before he could bend the biggest corporation on earth back toward its original incredible idea, relentless love, and away from its addiction to control. Since then the hierarchy, up to and including the remarkable man who now steers the ship, seems to have been more interested in conserving power than in correcting pride.

The priesthood, including the late public relations genius of a pope, has in general wished to protect the cherished idea of a paternal and pastoral church that led and taught its flock. Meanwhile the flock, at least in much of the West, increasingly found many of the men who had vowed to be their shepherds uninterested in and dismissive of what the flock itself felt and how its members lived.

Which is why in my lifetime millions of American Catholics, including me, have saluted the hierarchy with respect and often affection even as we steeled ourselves to make certain moral decisions based on our own tested experience of the world.

And then came revelations of rape and more rape, and of cowardly bishops and cardinals who with their lies let children be ruined in their parishes by twisted and troubled priests. How deep, we saw, was the squirming evil in the corporation expressly designed to fight against evil. "The smoke of Satan," as the American bishops themselves have said.

I have three small children; I was enraged. And I remain enraged, afraid, and bitter. The organization into which I was born, in which I was schooled, to which I have devoted much of my professional life, is revealed to be a place where men at the highest levels shut their eyes to the screams of children in the next room.

Yet this acid bath may heal the church, may scour it of its faults, and leave it the institution that little Angelo Roncalli dreamed of: a church, I pray quietly, that will be a stunning voice against poverty and hunger and greed and violence, a voice that can be heard over national and political and ethnic snarling, a chorus of brothers and sisters bound by the unreasonable faith that love will conquer bloodlust.

A clan, an idea, a force, an energy, a prayerful verb that reaches for its brothers and sisters among other faiths and creeds; that reunites with other Christian faiths and with its parent and root, Judaism; that links arms with the other faiths that sense the *One* over all; that joins hands with the faiths that chase the holy miracle of life and call it many names.

Possible? No. I am no fool.

Possible. Yes. I believe.

The men of the priesthood and hierarchy who betrayed the church are but a tiny percentage of the Catholic world. They cannot do permanent harm to a church that is made up of their vowed brothers and sisters who are faithful, loyal, gracious, and self-giving and of all of us — mothers, fathers, children, single people, gay and divorced and separated men and women, all the people in the fifteenth pew, and very many who never sit in pews at all but savor Christ's words in their hearts.

What will shatter, what I pray will shatter, is a culture of power in the Catholic Church — a culture the church has wrestled with for many centuries, because the church is a human construct draped on an incredible idea, and human constructs, as you and I know, are liable to violence and greed, craven cupidity, arrogance, lies.

I do not forget the early church, that band of brothers and sisters who formed community around the ludicrous idea that a young skinny intense devout poetic confusing dazzling Jew preaching love love love was Himself the distilled essence of the unimaginable Force that created all that is.

But they persisted in a dangerous and uncertain time and place. Choosing their own priests and electing their bishops from among themselves, they met in fields and forests, and steered clear, as best they could, of power and money, trying to focus on the young Jew's message and on the task of forging that wild message into a new peace, a new way of being, a revolution that could be carried in hearts to the ends of the earth.

Inevitably it took an organization to arrange that carrying, and no organization of human beings can persist for two thousand years without harboring sin and vice. And so as brave and as generous as the organization has been, it has also been murderous and cruel, responsible, in shameful spite of its divine inspirations, for much spilled blood, death, and human suffering. In its modern incarnation, the organization can be said to be egregiously mismanaged, with far too few managers, and just about all of them male and unmarried, and too many of them elderly. The organization is, despite its worldwide scope, headquartered in a vast ancient Italian castle where a cadre of mostly Italian men persist in trying to authoritatively manage the lives and loves and souls of a billion people in several hundred countries around the planet. The organization is, despite its own very public cry for openness — *aggiornamento* — forty years ago, in real ways closed to women, closed to gay people, closed to divorced people, closed to the very same sort of scattered group of wounded and yearning men and women who dispersed from Jerusalem to carry the news of a love that did not die.

But I suggest that this closed corporation is dying and being reborn before our eyes; it is crumbling and shattering and roiling and churning while something in its institutional heart is struggling to be born anew. I suggest that these days are the first days of the new church. I suggest that in this church, the Vatican becomes Buckingham Palace, a beloved and respected and necessary and nutritious element of Catholicism, but not an imperial headquarters, and certainly not in charge. I suggest that in this new church the pope will be elected not by cardinals but by worldwide acclamation of his people every bit as inspired by the Holy Spirit as their cardinals locked in a room together have been in the past. I suggest that in this new church synods of bishops will someday be the leaders of the faithful in their nations and districts, beholden to the people of God they have sworn to serve.

I suggest that dioceses and archdioceses may someday again elect their own priests and bishops in this new church, and that women will take their rightful places in the first ranks of teachers and pastors in the church.

I suggest that parishes and dioceses, already teetering financially, will become spiritual villages in large part devoted to schools, which are what raised up the American Catholic Church in the nineteenth and twentieth centuries.

I suggest that this church will welcome and celebrate its gay members with all its heart, not in the current manner of public acceptance and private disdain; and that it will welcome and celebrate its divorced and remarried members without aid of the clownish and Byzantine apparatus of annulment.

I suggest that the great legacy of John Paul II in this new church will not be his marginalization of women and insistence on central control, but his ferocious insistence that Christ's message can destroy totalitarian governments without smart bombs, that wars indicate failure of religious imagination, and that we are brothers and sisters with all people who pursue holiness.

I suggest that my church will always be a struggle and a mess, will always be a human yearning and failure, will always be striving and falling, will always be a house for wonder and woe, will never be what it wishes to be; but in years to come it will be closer to the spirit of its astounding and miraculous birth than it has been in two millennia.

The Catholic idea, all these years after Christ died and rose and his friends scattered around the world on their incredible public relations mission, remains stunning and unbelievable — and crucial. And the church, which eventually enfleshed that idea, and which has meant so much to so many, and so much to Western civilization, and saved so many souls and so many lives from despair, stands now at a crossroad the likes of which it has not faced since the Emperor Constantine saw a sword of fire in the sky and suddenly reconsidered the efficacy of massacring Christians.

This church will, in the years to come, either fall into dusty insignificance, or be reborn and resurrected in a creative, singing form we can as yet only dimly know; and I only hope and pray that I live to see this church, and to see that it matters more than it ever has.

~ 7 ~

Glow

Ann Wroe

I know what Hope looks like. Ever since childhood I've carried in my mind a picture, drawn from some children's encyclopedia, of Pandora opening her box. Out fly all the world's evils, fanged and clawed and leather-winged. They beat around the poor girl's head and stream away into the distance. But the trick is to notice Hope, as Pandora patently does not: a tiny, faintly glowing, winged sprite, huddled in a corner of the box.

Hope is ever pictured thus. It is not strong, but frail and small. It doesn't blaze like a beacon, but gives a glowworm's or an ember's light. Typically, it is buried under ash or hidden in darkness, a self-effacing thing. When we invoke Paul's splendid words, "Faith, hope, and love, all three," Hope almost vanishes in the dazzle of the others, like a pale third Muse between two radiant sisters in some festive procession.

Historians — and I am one by training — don't set much store by Hope. "The triumph of hope over experience" we say, and smirk, because experience is solid, knowable, and relentless, and Hope is a butterfly flitting weakly above it — or, more prosaically, Neville Chamberlain waving his white paper at Hendon Aerodrome in September 1938. Hope's victory, we know, is already doomed. By the time we begin to write the next chapter, Hope will have vanished.

In my catalogue of virtues, Hope holds an unsteady place anyway. After all, everyone hopes, and often for insubstantial and selfish things. I hope I can get home early after finishing this piece, and relax in the sun. I hope no one will notice if I slip off early. I hope there's some soup left downstairs, and that my colleagues won't have finished it. Larger hopes — for the boys' exam results, an important e-mail, that the dog may not be irretrievably lost — I often underpin with bits of superstition, such as crossing fingers and touching wood, as if I know Hope alone is not enough. St. Anthony is invoked too, a useful, busy, efficient saint, not so much to represent Hope as to reinforce it and help it out. Hope, indeed, has no saint, and can seem inert and inactive in my breast. But I have never yet been reduced to praying to St. Jude, the patron of hopeless cases, and therefore giving up entirely. There is always Hope, somewhere. There is never, in my life, a hopeless case.

Yet hope for what? From day to day, Hope can seem a most self-centered and almost guilty thing. Faith, by contrast, is either noble and Herculean — too much so for my grubby and ordinary daily life — or else involuntary, and therefore somewhat worrying to the rational side of me. It requires both more confidence than I can easily gather up, and more humility. As for Love, the be-all and end-all, I am simply incapable of doing all Love requires. I try and, in the meantime, I hope.

And that seems to be the core of the matter. Hope, more than anything else, characterizes my human existence. Despite faith's assurances and philosophy's suggestions, I do not know and cannot know my true nature and my fate. I feel comforted by Catholicism, but not made certain. If I were certain, I would presumably be in some blessed and exalted state in which Hope would no longer be needed. Instead, lost in the world's obscurity, I hope — and for the best.

Against the scale of the universe and my ignorance, it's small wonder that Hope can seem such a small, frail, almost pitiable thing. Inevitably, I return to that picture of Pandora in the crowd of evils, with only the tiniest gleam of light left behind in the box. To pit Hope against the world's miseries, the huge weight of doubt and the dark, seems foolish. Indeed, it can seem almost irresponsible. The gods who left Hope in the box were not, after all, famous for their thoughtfulness.

Yet I also believe quite different things of Hope: that it is vital, and it is strong. For in hoping, and acting on that hope, we can bring into being what we hope for. Hope is the virtue by which we idealize and create —

the landscape in which we build our visions. It is not just a matter of carrying hope, like a sort of pocket torch against the dark. It is a matter of using hope's strength to construct everything good, from a poem to a garden to a family to a city. Hope, it could be argued, is man's most fundamental motive force. The higher we aspire, the better we and the world can be.

Some of the best lines written about Hope come from the poet Shelley, whose inner life I have been exploring for the past few years. Shelley — less an atheist than an agnostic, despite his proud trumpeting of the former title — refused to believe, but insisted on hope. At the end of "Prometheus Unbound," his great poem of moral regeneration, he described the duty of all men and women:

> To suffer woes which Hope thinks infinite;
> To forgive wrongs darker than death or night;
> To defy Power, which seems omnipotent;
> To love, and bear; to hope til Hope creates
> From its own wreck the thing it contemplates...

I like now to think that the apparent weakness of Hope, its pallor and weariness, are illusions. Hope is a subversive and insidious thing. When called on, it can flare up in visions and encouragement. And when I see it as insignificant and fading, this is surely only because it has given almost everything, and is rallying to shine again.

～ 8 ～

At the Source
Paula Huston

People's stubborn commitment to Monday night meditation amazes me. Sometimes, though I live here, I barely
make it on time myself, have to scramble down the hill
from my studio, slip into clean clothes, and rush to the
barn before the first car pulls down the dirt lane. As group
members come quietly up the stairs to the loft, I am still
lighting the candles and turning on the twinkling lights
that let our neighbors know it's time to stop mowing,
weed-whacking, and running their leaf-blowers. They are
good about this, though some of them are nervous about
linking the terms "Christian" and "meditation."

In the Monday evening calm, with all the dormer windows open and the wing-shwish of band-tailed pigeons
settling themselves across the tops of the jack pines, we
sit, some of us on barley-filled Zen meditation pillows
called zafus, some on inches-high wooden benches, some
on straight-backed chairs. Together, we look like an ad-
vertisement for unity in diversity: our group includes a

hardware store owner, a marathon runner, a software designer, a prison guard, a nurse, a marriage counselor, an actress, and a handful of teachers.

Someone leads a brief evening Vespers service. Someone else says an opening prayer written by the London-based World Community of Christian Meditators. Eyes closed, we ask that God "open our hearts to the presence of the spirit" of his Son, that he "lead us into the mysterious silence" where his love is revealed to all who call, "Maranatha...Come, Lord Jesus." The chime sounds. We bow, then enter into the interior quiet that Trappist monk and scholar Andre Louf refers to as a "pit which has to be further and further excavated till we strike the water of the Spirit, bubbling up from the bottom of our heart."

This faithful group is one source of my hope in the twenty-first-century church, which has welcomed and embraced the rediscovery of Christianity's long-lost contemplative tradition.

Another source: twenty people on the far side of middle age, whose calendars bristle with dates and deadlines, meeting for some purely joyful, non-productive hours together. Inside the Cal Poly State University Newman Center meeting room, with its student-battered sofas and taco-stained rugs, the gold light of morning fills the air, briefly firing our clutch of mundane selves with icon-like glory. This day, instead of everlasting, weary-making busyness, our community of Camaldolese

Benedictine oblates, united by lay vows made at a nearby hermitage, gathers for the singing of Lauds, silent prayer, monk-led talks, a feast of wine and laughter, solitary time to walk and think, the sharing of the Eucharist.

As a group, we gather every three months, but at any given time at least one of us is making an individual pilgrimage up winding, precipitous Highway 1 to the north, connecting and reconnecting, like fond family members, with the twenty-five monks who live on a mountain above the sea. Afterward, made peaceful by silence and thanksgiving, a state of grace we ruefully understand won't stay with us for long, we return to our families and jobs, trying as best we can to reflect back what we've been given. Internationally, there are over five hundred of us oblates, a puzzling lay-to-monk ratio that is replicating itself in monasteries everywhere. Bruno Barnhart, for many years prior at New Camaldoli Hermitage, suggests that, in our time, monasteries may be acting as "watering holes" for the spiritually parched and sanctuaries for those made frantic by contemporary crazybusyness.

These faithful oblates — professors, hospice volunteers, choir directors, social workers, writers, clerks, and dental chairside assistants — are another sign of hope within the twenty-first-century church.

And yet another source: meeting my spiritual director, Fr. Isaiah, in the hermitage bookstore for our monthly talk about my frequently troublous love affair with God. As we walk down the mountain, he with his vaguely

Hasidic-looking sun hat and Mt. Athos–style beard and I in my shades, I admit to pridefully concealed heart-wounds, lashing anger, and nihilistic broodiness that I can hardly bear to record in my own journal. Far, far below us California's Highway 1 snakes along the cliffs, and a thousand feet below that, the great Pacific rolls restlessly against the land mass in its path. A blue jay follows us, hopping from redwood branch to oak twig to rock and eyeing the beard-thicket with a cautious, speculative interest.

> *Our lives on this earth are both achingly beautiful and discouragingly corrupt.*

By the end of our hike Fr. Isaiah has managed to bless every one of the subtle seductions that oppress me, turning them into golden gifts and opportunities. Then we go into the church, where he pulls on his priestly alb and stole, and I make my formal confession and am once again, this time sacramentally, absolved and blessed. Both the blessing and the alchemical transformation of sin into gift make it possible for me to meet with other sorrowful or confused or woefully tempted people and to render, I hope, the same life-giving, light-bearing service. For as spiritual director Carolyn Gratton points out, people these days are seeking out soul friends such as Fr. Isaiah in "overwhelming numbers and for reasons beyond counting."

Given the spectacular display that evil is making in the world right now, this vast, delicate movement toward a more intimate relationship with the Holy One gives me great hope indeed for the twenty-first-century church.

Thus it is that for me, in my small life, the church of our time is neither moribund, as certain understandably weary warriors for change would have it, nor corrupted beyond repair, as those who have been victims of institutionally sheltered sin might with all justification believe. Instead, it is as pregnant with hope as Mary headed for Bethlehem. The Spirit is moving across the land, and people electrified by the brush of its wing are turning, as naturally as one is turned by the wind, to our two-thousand-year-old Catholic repository of spiritual wisdom — to the saints and the sacraments and the spiritual disciplines, to the virtues and to prayer — for stabilizing reassurance that what is happening to them is both very real and very good.

Those who wrote the documents of Vatican II must have intuited the spiritual whirlwind that now spins and spits fire among us. It was they who set aside the old image of the impregnable Roman monolith — an impediment to the free action of the Holy Spirit if ever there was one — and reminded us that we are instead a "pilgrim church and a pilgrim people," willing and eager to move forward into mystery. And thus we the church become the seedbed of hope, for it is this Christian *status viatoris,* which Josef Pieper defines as the "condition of being on the way," that is hope's very basis.

For our lives on this earth are both achingly beautiful and discouragingly corrupt. Unless we remember the "not yet" context in which we abide, we will despair. Conversely, if in self-defense we fantasize that we have already arrived, we presume too much and hope is killed within us, we who are meant to live as the Body of Christ in this troubled world. Instead, we are to poise our lives on a "certain glad expectancy of God." We are to set our feet firmly on the fact that "hope does not disappoint, because the love of God has been poured out into our heart through the holy Spirit that has been given to us" (Rom. 5:5). When we live in hope this way, everything — including a twenty-first-century church that suffers under the wounds of sin, scandal, and profound internal disagreement — quite naturally becomes gift and opportunity.

Just as Fr. Isaiah keeps ever so gently reminding me.

❧ 9 ❧

Resistance

Richard K. Taylor

I have not come easily to my feelings about what we Catholics must now do, and the radical measures we must take, in order to rekindle hope in our church. I am a convert from Quakerism who entered joyfully into communion with the Roman Catholic Church in 1982, at age forty-nine. Being Catholic has blessed, inspired, spiritually enriched, and challenged me. I love the Mass and often find myself weeping during it, just as I did twenty-five years ago when I first experienced what it means to receive the Body of Christ. As a person who loves Jesus, I appreciate deeply the unabashedly Christ-centeredness of Catholicism, in which every symbol and ceremony points us to our Savior. The Sacrament of Reconciliation and my relationships with (now six) spiritual directors have strengthened my relationship with Christ, brought light into all the dark corners of my soul, and assured me of forgiveness. Nothing except the Bible has so deepened my spiritual life as reading the lives of the saints and the great Catholic devotional classics, like *The Imitation of Christ.*

My multiracial, inner-city parish in Philadelphia has given me a supportive Christian community that I treasure. I am proud to be part of a parish and a broader church that embraces people of all cultures, races, ages, classes, and nationalities. When I volunteer in our parish prison ministry, I feel solidarity with the tens of millions of Catholics around the world who care for "the least of these." As I work with our peace and justice ministry, I am aware of the multitudes of Catholics who labor to prevent war, protect the unborn, care for the environment, support human rights, and free the oppressed. Catholic faith has inspired us to see Christ in the face of the poor and to work for a more just and peaceful world.

To the surprise of some of my friends, I appreciate the church's teaching magisterium. I believe that it is largely responsible (along with the Holy Spirit, of course) for upholding the truth of Christ over two thousand years. I am put off when our leaders act with seeming arrogance or heavy-handedness, or don't appear to practice what they teach. Nevertheless, they help keep us on track. They help us honor Jesus' prayer "that they may all be one."

Coming from Quakerism, in which laypeople take charge of congregational life, I also appreciate how my gifts have been affirmed and utilized in the church. At the invitation of two cardinals, I've served on two archdiocesan commissions. I had mutually respectful exchanges with Cardinal Bernardin and Cardinal Krol and with Bishop Gumbleton as the bishops were writing their famous peace pastoral issued in 1983. In my parish, I have been a staff member, a Rite of Christian Initiation for Adults (RCIA) teacher, a co-founder of our peace ministry, a leader in our racial healing process, and a welcomer of new parishioners.

Crucial to my journey to Catholicism was the upbeat witness of a growing circle of Catholic friends who prayed with me, answered my questions, and shared the deep meaning of Catholicism in their own lives. They were realistic about Catholic shortcomings but were filled with hope and enthusiasm for the positive direction in which the Vatican II–inspired church seemed to be moving in the early 1980s.

For a great many of these friends, this hope has been dashed. Some have joined Protestant denominations. Others have left the church to seek alternative spiritual paths. Others say they are hanging on to Catholicism by their fingernails. They say it is heart-wrenching to be Catholic these days. Everywhere they turn are painful realities that have undercut or even destroyed their Catholic faith. Sex abuse scandals. Bishops' cover-ups. Retrogressive changes in the liturgy. The movement to roll back Vatican II. The attacks that gay and lesbian Catholics have to endure as the church they love describes their sexual expression as depraved and disordered. The fading hope that women's leadership gifts can ever be expressed in ordination. The unwillingness of most parish and diocesan leaders to be financially transparent and accountable to those whose contributions sustain the church. The closed-mindedness of the hierarchy to questions like optional celibacy or a married clergy. The princely lifestyles of church leaders, so unlike that of Jesus.

"The church will never change," my Catholic (and former Catholic) friends say, "at least not in our lifetime. Why wait around in painful longing for something that may never come?" If we are to retain — or regain — hope in the church, I believe that concerned Catholics must develop a movement for profound and far-reaching reforms to address these concerns.

I know that the church has experienced such reforms in the past. We no longer torture heretics or insist that the Earth is the center of the universe. In modern times, the church has made an amazing turnaround by confessing its mistake in holding the Jewish people responsible for Christ's death. Truly remarkable reforms — in liturgy, attitudes toward the Bible, etc. — have occurred in the last fifty years.

◆ ◆ ◆

But how can reform happen in today's church, where so many reform groups feel ignored, rebuffed, and up against a brick wall of hierarchical resistance? As I search for an answer, I inevitably draw upon my Quaker background in peaceful social change, my lifelong study of nonviolence, and my participation in many successful nonviolent movements. I recall especially the privilege of having been a member of Dr. Martin Luther King Jr.'s field staff during the civil rights movement.

A fundamental insight of nonviolence theory is that unjust structures or practices can exist only so long as people go along with them. When people resist and refuse to cooperate with injustice or wrong — and are willing to bear the consequences of their refusal — these bad practices and structures fall. The British colonialists, despite their monopoly on power in India, could not turn back the nonviolent resistance and noncooperation movement led by Mahatma Gandhi. Similarly, the Filipino dictator Ferdinand Marcos could not hold on to his power in the face of massive street demonstrations, often led by priests, nuns, and seminarians.

When my discouraged Catholic friends say, "The church will never change," I sometimes challenge them with the simple phrase, "But what if . . . ?"

"What if" a mere one-half of 1 percent of American Catholics (320,000 people) stood in prayer outside the U.S. Conference of Catholic Bishops' annual meeting, insisting that the laity (99.99 percent of all Catholics) have a meaningful voice in the bishops' deliberations?

"What if" Catholics, in a diocese whose leaders refuse to open secret files on sex abusers, were to flood the diocesan office with thousands of keys "in case they need help unlocking their files"?

"What if" Catholics, in a national campaign for church financial accountability, were to withhold their contributions to their bishops' Annual Appeal and instead send their money directly to the charities needing support, as has been done by Voice of the Faithful affiliates in Dayton and Long Island?

I do not think these visions of large-scale resistance are unrealistic. Recall how the civil rights movement began, not with 250,000 Americans marching on Washington in 1963, but with individuals like Rosa Parks in 1955, refusing to relinquish her bus seat to a white man in Montgomery, Alabama.

Black citizens back then rankled under the indignities of segregation. Creative organizers took that justifiable ire and showed how it could be transformed into creative, strong, loving, nonviolent direct-action campaigns. Their movement overcame entrenched, carefully rationalized, centuries-old structures of white supremacy and, in an amazingly short time, dismantled the whole system of legal segregation. Maybe American Catholicism is like Montgomery and Little Rock in the 1950s, waiting for people to learn about nonviolence, to get trained in organizing methods, and to use these to mobilize millions of Catholics for reform.

10

Eternal Spring
Peggy Rosenthal

I like to picture hope as the majestic French Catholic poet
Charles Péguy does. In his book-length poem *The Portal of the Mystery of Hope* (Eerdmans, 1996), he casts the
theological virtue of hope as an effervescent girl with a
child's unbounded confidence in renewal. At the Corpus
Christi procession, though the grown-ups get tired, hope
is "never tired":

> She's twenty steps ahead of them, like a little
>   puppy....
> She has fun with the garlands in the procession.
> She plays with the flowers and the leaves
> As if they weren't sacred garlands.
> She plays by jumping on top of the foliage
> The freshly cut, freshly gathered foliage that's
>   strewn about.
> She doesn't stay in place during the stations.
> She'd rather keep marching. Keep moving ahead.
> Keep jumping. Keep dancing. She's so happy.

She doesn't spare herself; and likewise, she doesn't
　　spare others either.
She makes us return twenty times to the same
　　place.
Which is generally a place of disappointment
(Earthly disappointment.)
Earthly wisdom is none of her business.
She doesn't calculate like we do.

Hope sees what has not yet been and what will be.
She loves what has not yet been and what will be.

Now the little girl hope
Is she who forever begins.

This birth
Perpetual birth.

Absolutely nothing at all
Holds except for the young child
Hope,
Because of she who continually begins again and
　　forever promises,
Who guarantees everything.

Hope makes pure water from impure water,
Young water from old water.

Springs from old water.
Fresh souls from old souls.

Young mornings from old evenings.
Clear souls from troubled souls.

Rising souls from setting souls.
Flowing souls from stagnant souls.

It's from impure water that she makes an eternal
    spring....
The eternal spring of my [God's] grace itself.

Where do I find the spirit of this bubbly, ever-renewing
hope?

I find hope in the communities of nuns, all over the
country and the world, who are boundless in their creative energy for ministering to God's people in need.
These women "don't stay in place during the stations."
They "keep moving ahead, jumping, dancing" with Christ
who is Lord of the Dance. They have "fun with the
garlands in the procession / as if they weren't sacred garlands." They make "flowing souls from stagnant souls" —
souls stagnant in the despair of poverty and oppression. They are the hope who "makes pure water from
impure water"; literally so in the case of a ministry of
the School Sisters of Notre Dame (Milwaukee Province)
called "Global Partners: Running Waters," which orga-
nizes and finds funders for projects that bring clean water
into Latin American villages. I learned of Global Partners while experiencing a creative ministry of another

religious community: the solidarity tours of Central America and Eastern Europe called GATE (Global Awareness Through Experience), sponsored by the Franciscan Sisters of Perpetual Adoration.

Where do I find the spirit of this bubbly, ever-renewing hope?

I find hope in the multitude of inventive projects to empower the poor that I visited on a GATE tour of Guatemala. In these projects — initiated by lay Catholics as well as religious communities and clergy — lives the hope who "doesn't spare herself," who makes "rising souls from setting souls," "who continually begins again." Hope is embodied, for instance, in a young Catholic laywoman from Maine named Hanley Denning, who happened upon the Guatemala City garbage dump and was appalled to see swarms of children picking garbage instead of going to school. In the hope that "doesn't calculate like we do," Hanley established the cheery, joyous refuge called "Safe Passage," offering the children education, meals, health care, green grass, and flowers. Safe Passage grows the flowers for hope to play with in the Corpus Christi procession.

I find hope in laypeople like Jack Jezreel. Pondering the Gospels and our century of Catholic social teaching, Jack was struck that justice for the poor is at the core of our faith. Infused by the hope who leaps ahead — "who forever begins" and extravagantly "guarantees everything" — Jack invented JustFaith ministries, the parish-based immersion process that is converting Catholics throughout the country (more than ten thousand already) to the solidarity with the poor to which God calls us.

I find hope in the JustFaith national sponsors: the U.S. bishops' Catholic Campaign for Human Development, Catholic Relief Services, Catholic Charities. These organizations give the institutional church a good name. For countless of God's children, they make "young mornings from old evenings."

I find hope in the parish I've worshiped with for nearly a quarter-century, a true eucharistic community, where we know Christ in the breaking of the bread and go forth from Mass to love and serve our God in one another and in our neighbors. But what happens to hope when our very existence as a eucharistic community is threatened? While many, so many, people called to the vocation of priesthood are kept out because of their gender or marital state, our eucharistic communities are broken apart because there is no priest to break the bread through which we know Christ. Can hope go forth dancing in the Corpus Christi procession when there's no longer a procession, no longer the sacrament of Corpus Christi leading us from our church altar?

I find hope in the priests and bishops of my acquaintance who know that their own vocation will be enriched when women share in it. They do all they can to enable the fullness of the Christ life for those in their pastoral care. They live the hope who "sees what has not yet been and what will be," who "loves what has not yet been and what will be."

I find hope in creative theologians like Elizabeth Johnson and James Alison, who voice a "faith beyond resentment" (Alison's phrase), a refusal to mirror the exclusionary language of a hierarchy that marginalizes them as women or gays. In hope, they "return twenty times to the same place / Which is generally a place of disappointment / (Earthly disappointment.)" Yet, in hope, even this is a place of delight, of renewal. Hope won't stay put. "She'd rather keep jumping. Keep dancing. She's so happy."

Is hope deluded in her happiness? No, because the source of her bubbling energy, her "perpetual birth," is — says God in Péguy's poem — "the eternal spring of my grace itself."

⮜ 11 ⮞

Cause and Effect
Peter Kreeft

"The nature of hope and its sources and uses in our time" is the topic I am to write about. The wording mentions three of Aristotle's "four causes." This is fortunate because no matter what topic you ask a philosopher to write about, you can expect it to be structured by Aristotle's "four causes," which is one of the most useful and commonsensical ways of structuring our writing about *anything* because it mirrors the structure of *everything* in the universe. (1) The "formal cause" is the essential form, nature, or definition; (2) the "material cause" is the content, or raw material; (3) the "efficient cause" is the source, agent, or maker; and (4) the "final cause" is the end or use or good, of anything. So what are the four causes of Christian hope in our time?

1. The question of the nature or "formal cause" of hope is not about our changing times but about hope's unchanging essence. Nothing ever loses or changes its

essence, though it can lose or change any of its accidental qualities. So what is the essence of Christian hope?

In ordinary language today the word is often used as a vague synonym for a feeling of optimism. But in Christian theology hope is a *virtue*, and virtues are not feelings (though their matter, or raw material, includes feelings) because feelings in themselves are neither virtuous nor vicious. We are directly responsible for our virtues, because they are under our control, they are freely chosen by repeated acts that create good or bad habits; but we are not responsible for our feelings because they arise in us without our direct control. Virtues are good habits; vices are bad habits. We all have some of both.

Faith, hope, and charity are "theological" virtues because their source and end is God. So the theological virtue of "hope" means hope in God, not in self, or humankind, or the world, or the future. These other hopes all may or may not be good things, but they are not guaranteed, and they are not the theological virtue of hope. Hope means something very simple: faith in God directed to the future, faith in God's promises. "God said it, I believe it, and that settles it," the famous "Suthun' Babdist" formula, is really not far off the mark. It explains the power of that line in the Catholic funeral ceremony: "in the *sure and certain* hope of the resurrection." The resurrection is equally present to the first century, the twenty-first century, and the last century, whenever that will be.

2. The material content of Christian hope is Christ. *"In him* are hid all the treasures" (Col. 2:3). Our hope is a blank check we give to God. Our trust in God is based on Christ, on the fact that ever since Christ made his astonishing love known, we can know that "God will meet *all* your needs according to his glorious riches in Christ Jesus" (Phil. 4:19), and that therefore *"all* things work together for good to them that love God" (Rom. 8:28). That is why St. Paul says that all the goods of this world are as *skubala* compared with Christ (Phil. 3:4–8). The old King James Version dared to translate that Greek word literally: "dung."

Christ did not promise his followers success in this world. Just the opposite: he said, "in the world you shall have tribulation. But be of good cheer: I have overcome the world" (John 16:33). I cannot think of a single canonized saint who had a life of riches, ease, comfort, and admiration in the world. Ten of the twelve apostles were martyrs. Christian hope is to be with Christ on the Cross, not that he will come down from the Cross (Matt. 27:39–44). Thus Christian hope has almost nothing in common with worldly hope — according to Christ himself. This is not "medieval," or "Evangelical," or "Fundamentalist," or "conservative." It is not a particular "party line" within Christianity. It is Christianity. It is Christ's own promise. It includes thorns.

But it also includes deep joy. The joy that comes from being with Christ, even on the Cross, is far greater than any pain. St. Catherine of Genoa said that the joy of purgatory is far greater than the pain, even though the pain is greater than any earthly pain, because Christ is there purging us. And St. Teresa said that the most painful life on earth, looked at from the viewpoint of heaven, will be seen to be no more than one night in an inconvenient hotel. Christians believe that, and hope for that. Christian hope is an investment in the bank of divine love.

3. Where does it come from? What is its efficient cause? It seems like "joy without a cause." But everything that happens, no matter how mysterious, must have a cause.

It does not come from human wisdom, optimism, goodwill, self-acceptance, or enlightenment. Nor does it come from folly, pessimism, superstition, ignorance, credulity, self-loathing, or other psychopathologies. It comes from God. It is a supernatural gift, one of the primary gifts of the Holy Spirit. We can't work it up within ourselves, although we can, alas, work up deceptive imitations of it.

If you do not believe this, if you are hard-headed and empirical and want data before you believe in this heavenly miracle, I say good for you, and I will tell you exactly where to go to get that data. Go to Mother Teresa's Missionaries of Charity in the Dorchester neighborhood of Boston. Be with them for a day. You will not see where the joy comes from, but you will see the joy in their whole being; and you will see where this joy does *not* come from:

you will see the total lack of all the identifiable worldly sources of joy in their Spartan lives.

Actually, you *can* see where their joy comes from. I asked one of them that question when I was there. (They asked me to speak to them. I have no idea what I said, because I remember only what they said to me. They didn't say it with speeches. They said it with their eyes, smiles, tone of voice, body language.) She answered my question very simply: "Follow our eyes." They look right at you, and into you, but that was not what she meant. When they look at you, and speak to you, it seems as if Another is looking at you too, and speaking to you, and this is because their eyes spend literally hours a day looking at Christ. When the nun said, "Follow our eyes," she was looking at the crucifix above the altar where Christ was present, really present, body and blood, soul and divinity, hidden under the appearances of bread and wine. They looked at him twenty-four hours a day. They let him look at them, and through them at us. That was their habit. And their secret of joy was scandalously simple: that look was joy because that look was love, infinite love, Christ's love, "love divine, all loves excelling, joy of heaven to earth come down."

All their vocations are from Latin America and India. Western women are for the most part too sophisticated, too attached to the world to give it up for that kind of joy. That's why you don't often see those deep smiles in

America. You see them most on faces in places like Hospice or Rosie's Place. I rarely see them in our churches. The smiles there are polite and conventional. But the smiles I'm talking about are imported from lands that are more open to imports from heaven. We are too concerned with securing our borders against those immigrants, especially "lower-class," simple-minded immigrants, like Jesus. (He wouldn't get a Green Card today.)

4. Which brings us to the last of the four causes of hope, the "final cause." What is hope's end or purpose or goal? What is hope's hope?

It is in the sky, though it begins in the earth. Hope is like the energy that moves the stem of the flower to grow upward, from its roots (which are like faith) to its fruits (which are like love). It is the energy that moves us toward our true end, which is God and the life of God and our participation in the life of God, which is the life of divine love. And that participation begins now. If the plant is not planted in earthly pots, it will not produce heavenly fruit. That is the reason you can see this joy in some lives and faces now.

And here is the best thing about Jesuit spirituality: the insistence of finding God in all things, people, places, and times *now*. (Read Teilhard de Chardin's *The Divine Milieu* to catch this great vision.) It is why I am happy to be a part of a Jesuit institution, and why I hope it never forgets its roots.

Does this mean I am optimistic that the twenty-first-century will see clear, public progress for the Catholic Church in America? Does it mean we will learn from our millstone-sized mistakes (see Luke 17:2) and climb up to the vision of John Paul II's "theology of the body" instead? Does it mean a "second spring" as Newman hoped?

God only knows, not I. But I know this: that the answer to that question is up to us. For as "The Little Flowers of St. Francis" says, "Who, thinkest thou, is the more willing: God to give grace or we to receive it?" Leon Bloy wrote: "Life offers only one tragedy, in the end: not to have been a saint," and William Law tells us the sole root of this tragedy: "If you will consult your heart in silence and honesty you must discover that the only reason you are not as pious as the primitive Christians is that you never wholly wanted to be."

The future of the church in the twenty-first century and in any century, in America and in any country, is dependent on its saints. Saints are the flowers of hope. Saints alone can save the world. Saints are little Christs.

Be one.

~ 12 ~

On the Way
Paul Elie

There are four hundred churches in Rome, and San Giuseppe della Lungara has got to be one of the ordinariest. The Counter-Reformation front shoehorned into a block of apartments; the iron banister bent into submission by twenty generations of old hands; the pair of green doors at the top of chipped and slanted stone steps blackened by exhaust from passing *motorini* — all are standard, and grim enough to banish any illusions about the vitality of the city and the church headquartered there.

The right door is held open by a loop of string. Past it is a plain pine booth of a vestibule, the knots in the wood an oddly rustic touch amid the soot and stone. You push a small door till a coiled spring strains open, and go in.

Inside, this church is cool and dark, musty like an unfinished basement, and so deserted as to seem abandoned. There are no windows, no chandeliers, only some spotlights at the corners just bright enough to show what is where. A number of wood-and-glass dioramas depicting scenes in the life of Christ protrude like bird-houses overhead. To each side and up front — "up at the holy end," as Philip Larkin put it — are altars with ropes swagged across them, museum-style. There are no signs of recent life here: no stray missals or dried palm fronds, no tracts or bulletins or collection envelopes, no left-behind umbrellas or wads of gum or children's toys or printed bulletins reporting on how many people came to church last Sunday.

Even as old churches go, this one is dispiriting, at least by the usual measures. Yet it became for me a place of hope during the bright spring days when a new pope was elected — became a reason for hope when that virtue, grounded more than any of the others in human weakness and dependence, was being crowded out by triumphalism on one side and dismay on the other.

I happened upon the church the first time on the Saturday after the conclave. Sent by the *Atlantic,* I had been in Rome two weeks earlier to attend John Paul's funeral, staying in a pilgrim house in the old historic center. Now I returned for a long weekend to see Joseph Ratzinger — the name Benedict hadn't taken hold yet — invested as pope and to attend, with several thousand others, his first press conference. I arrived that Saturday morning with just enough time to gain entry to a friend's vacant apartment in Trastevere, disinter a suit from a garment bag, and walk the mile to the Vatican along the via della Lungara, a narrow road set in the shadow of the Lungotevere, the tree-lined boulevard that runs along the Tiber.

In fact, I had a little more than enough time, and that I knew I did — that, after ten trips to Rome, I knew my way around the city — brought a pleasure much like the high brought on by lack of sleep, strong coffee, and Mediterranean morning light; and it was as if to redeem this pleasure that I ducked into the church whose green door stood open.

In the darkness, I was at once calmed and moved. Here was a church that — rare thing in Rome — was a church and nothing more: not the site of a saint or a refashioned pagan temple or the base of a religious order or the titular church of a prominent cardinal. It was a Roman church reduced to essences. It offered the meditatory aids associated — often in sinister ways — with the church of Rome, as the controversialists once called it. The dioramas dramatizing episodes in Christ's passion were out of reach but not out of sight, and it was clear that they had been expertly constructed. The roped-off altars were fronted by signs warning QUESTO ALTARE E'ALLARMATO — THIS ALTAR IS ALARMED, and yet they looked like altars in a Christian church, not Noguchi tables or xylophones. Here was a church for — well, for what I was doing now: kneeling and bowing my head and praying for the Lord's guidance in the work I had come to Rome to do.

Benedict was invested as pope, and I returned to Rome once more, this time settling in Trastevere with my family to write an article about how he had come to occupy the papal office. On foot, the via della Lungara is the most direct route from Trastevere to the Vatican, and I passed that old church nearly every morning in the weeks to follow, on the way to appointments with members of the Curia. As often as not, I went inside — computer in backpack, can of lemon soda protruding from pants pocket — and conceived a quick prayer.

It was some weeks before I learned the name of the church, and its translation: something like St. Joseph's in the Road that Runs Along, or St. Joe's on the Way.

What drew me back to that particular church then, and what draws me back to it now as a sign of hope? At the time, the nature of its attraction seemed obvious. In my reporting, I was passing through some of the most exalted spots in Rome: St. Peter's Basilica, the old monastic churches on the Aventine Hill, the mosaic-bedecked basilica of Santa Maria in Trastevere. But St. Joe's-on-the-Way was a "regular" church, one not burdened by symbolic greatness. And it was an empty, quiet, peaceful church — one where, even more than in the perfectly austere spaces of Santa Sabina and the like, it was possible to feel oneself in communion with Catholics worldwide, the living and the dead, and at the same time to feel alone with God.

Certainly its ordinariness was part of its appeal. But surely there was more to it than that.

Over time, on those morning walks from Trastevere to the Vatican, I realized that the church is halfway between the two districts — the one an old working people's redoubt, now a bohemian quarter, marked by a delicate late medieval arch; the other the seat of the church and the magnet for pilgrims from all over the world, marked by a broad stone arch set into the brown brick of the wall that is the border of Vatican territory. The road that runs between these two arches, which stand steadfastly at its ends as if erected out of children's blocks, was one of the first roads laid out in the Italian Renaissance, planned to offer the pilgrim a straight shot to St. Peter's; and in the centuries to follow it became one of the most traveled routes in the Christian world.

Today, though, the road to and from Vatican City is the Lungotevere, a broad boulevard built in the Mussolini era, which looms like a cliff over the neighborhood. Alongside this road, in the shadow of it, the via della Lungara has the feel of an alley or service road — buckled, grimy, made clamorous by the engines of small trucks and military vehicles and shortcut-seeking motorbikes. Just as the Tiber, once a flowing river, is now more like a catch basin for Rome's runoff, so the via della Lungara is a drain for traffic sloughed off by the more scenic Lungotevere.

Likewise the church of St. Joseph on the Road that
Runs Along. For centuries, it served pilgrims en route
to St. Peter's. Now I suspect it serves mainly people
from the neighborhood — a neighborhood that, like Italy
as a whole, claims fewer observant Catholics with each
passing year.

Over time, my work writing about the life of the
church in Rome had made a pilgrim of me, and over
time the via della Lungara and the church on it came
to suggest something important about the pilgrimage.
Left behind, the church had also been left untouched by
the forces usually taken for signs of life in the Catholic world — and taken for news by the people who write
about the church. Save for the orientation of the high
altar, it had not been renewed by Vatican II, for as far
as I could tell it had no windows to open. Nor had it
been restored by John Paul II, on whose watch Rome's
more illustrious churches were made to sparkle again,
the better to symbolize the restoration of Catholic orthodoxy. Its spot at the midpoint between Trastevere and the
Vatican was no metaphor for a contest between worldly
playground and clerical fortress; the warning signs and
alarms at the altars were not figures for the exclusion of
women or married men from the priesthood, just pre-
cautionary measures put in place so the church could be
left open.

And open it was, morning after morning. There it
stood, a survivor, its door held back with that piece of

string even when nobody was around, so that it might witness the life passing before it — and welcome a pilgrim from time to time.

In the books about the church written when the gulf with Protestantism was widest, the church of Rome is characterized by its fixity. The church is an absolute, a feature on the landscape, a port (as Newman had it) where every ship ought to call.

I remember reading the *Apologia* as a young man in the 1980s and being left bewildered, for the church of my experience was characterized not by fixity, but by change. It was to this sense of constant and tumultuous change that John Paul sought to respond. But to have spent any time in Rome in recent years is to have become aware that the era of John Paul, too, was characterized by change in the church. The ever greater reach of the pope's itinerary; the serial drama of the Jubilee; the reining in of even the most temperate postconciliar initiatives; the reshaping of the cardinalate so as to make it at once geographically diverse and theologically uniform; the melodrama of John Paul's last illness and the hullabaloo over his death — all would have surprised his predecessors. Avery Dulles has said that each epoch in the church's life can be seen as having a single overriding preoccupation, and that the twentieth century was the "century of the church" — in which questions about the nature of the church were *the* questions for Catholic believers. If that is the case, under John Paul it was the case right up to the end.

Against this background that small, dark, empty church on the grimy old byway seemed to me — and seems to me now — a reason for hope, for it is a sign of life that is not a sign of change. There it stands, unoccupied, unsupervised, but still open — no small thing, as those of us in the big cities of the United States now have special reason to know.

It may sound as if, in idealizing such a church, I am hoping for a Catholic Church that is fixed and unchanging. But I don't think that is the case. I'd say that I hope, rather, for a church in which the life of faith is not so often conflated with the yearning for change in the church, whether as a relaxation or a restoration.

I would hope, in other words, for the "century of the church" to be over, and for our life as Catholics to be defined by some other preoccupation. Maybe we are now in the century of history, as Catholics undertake the "pilgrimage in time" called for by Vatican II in the sixties and called forth by the collapse of communism two decades later. Maybe it is now the century of women, as the presence of women in the church, already so unmistakable, shapes the church's life in the face of efforts to the contrary. Maybe it will be the century of the church as the "salt of the earth," in which Catholics go forward together with other Christians, and with Jews and Muslims and people of other faiths, and Catholicism recognizes that it is, at least sociologically, one religion among many. Each of these would bring change — but as an effect of

Catholic lives fully and faithfully lived, rather than as an end in itself.

I would hope, that is, for the church in search of itself to find itself as the church on the way.

I knelt in the back of the church once more. The roar of motorbikes came through the open door, engines revving for the straightaway. The church itself was quiet, however. I considered the darkness at the other end. I might have prayed just then for the century of the church to pass. But I had plenty else to pray for. I lowered my head, lofted a prayer in the general direction of heaven, and set out for my appointment at the Vatican a little later than I had expected.

Part Two

LOVE

❧ 13 ❧

Josie
Melissa Musick Nussbaum

The only really effective apologia for Christianity comes down to two arguments, namely, the saints which the church has produced and the art which has grown in its womb. — Pope Benedict XVI

When her obituary ran in the local newspaper, the words made Josie sound small, her death of no particular matter: Colorado native, retired from food service at Penrose Hospital, preceded in death by her husband, survived by her daughter and grandchildren. Services to be held at St. Mary's Cathedral on Saturday morning. There was not a mention of Josie's green chile. She made it the fiery way she learned in the valley, San Luis–style — roasted green chiles and pork, no heat-absorbing potatoes. People who don't know better use potatoes. Her sister-in-law uses tomatoes, but, then, as much as Josie loved her, she wasn't from San Luis.

At church dinners, we searched the tables for Josie's chile. We angled to get a batch for Christmas. Women knew to go easy on the mascara before eating her chile. You needed cold beer for washing it down and extra napkins for mopping it up.

She made green chile for funeral dinners and parish potlucks and for the catechumens she sponsored on their often surprising journeys into the church. Josie had learned to cook it as a child. When Josie's mother was pregnant with the youngest of the five Martinez children, her husband died. After she gave birth, Mrs. Martinez went to work and left the little ones in Josie's care. Josie was eight years old.

Josie's baby brother remembers getting in trouble with the other neighbor children. Their parents felt free to scold him, the fatherless boy whose mother was always gone. He remembers little Josie coming out of the house, angry, telling them to mind their own boys and she would mind hers.

Josie grew up and married and had a baby and went to work as a cook at the local Catholic hospital. Green chile was never on the patients' menu.

Josie went to daily Mass. When her husband was dying, she would linger after Mass to ask the priest, "Will you come to my house? Will you bring communion to my husband?"

The priest came. After a while he suggested that Josie do what she had always done, and feed her husband from her own hands. She was surprised, and a little scared.

"Could I do this?" she asked herself.

"Am I worthy?" she asked the priest.

"Well, yes and no," he answered, "just like me. Able, yes, and willing. And unworthy, too, but called all the same."

Virtue is a way of living, a way of being in the world. A just woman does justice. A merciful man forgives.

So it was Josie who gave her husband the viaticum, the bread for his final journey. After his death, she continued that work, feeding the people of St. Mary's. She stood down in the kitchen cooking and at the altar pouring wine. She stood before us on Sundays, her hands filled with bread for the hungry, her mouth opened to give good news, "The Body of Christ," here, now, for you.

It seemed right to gather at St. Mary's for Josie's funeral and be fed.

I don't know what Josie expected out of life, what she dreamed as a girl. I doubt her early dreams were realized. Her childhood was marked by death and poverty and adult responsibilities. She was not educated. She was not rich. She was not famous. She was not powerful. She did not have "interesting work." Her life was hard. But if you had asked me what hope looks like, I would have pointed to Josie, and, if you had asked me how it tastes, I would have handed you a bowl of her green chile.

Hope, along with faith and love, is a theological virtue, but a virtue is not only, or primarily, an idea. Virtue is a way of living, a way of being in the world. A just woman does justice. A merciful man forgives. Loving men and women love.

Hope is a longing for God, a way of life in which one longs to be in company with the beloved.

Hope is a longing for God, a way of life in which one longs to be in company with the beloved. It is living in invitation to God, "Please. You are welcome here."

We learn the hospitality of hope the way we learn all hospitality — by receiving it and watching to see how it's done. We catch hope, just as we catch walking and talking and the measles, from other people.

St. Paul speaks of "reliable witnesses," of people we can wisely imitate. "If you want to live in hope, if you want to live in Christ," I can imagine Paul saying, "watch Josie, and do what she does. Go with her to visit the sick, clean with her and cook with her and pray with her and you will learn all you need."

We look for them everywhere — the reliable witnesses, the sturdy ones who know how to build a fence and soothe a child, who know the difference between the poisonous weed and the nourishing root. We look for them every day, the ones who can show us what is worth carrying on the journey and what will only weigh us down.

Life in hope, life in Christ — a brother doing the dishes and singing as he scrubs, a sister wiping a soiled backside, careful with her touch — is hard work, hard learned.

Late in her life, Josie became an RCIA sponsor, walking with the catechumens on their path to the baptismal font and the table. Like dancers learning a new step, they needed someone to follow. Josie's steps were sure.

Some of us still make her chile, trying to cook it Josie's way. All of us tell her story. She was a saint, whose icon would surely show a wreath of green chiles wound through her thick, gray hair. Like the catechumens she taught, we try to remember her steps, try to catch the rhythm and the flow. If we can just follow her, placing our feet carefully in her deep prints, we have hope, hope that we can follow Josie home.

∾ 14 ∾

Pilgrims
Lawrence S. Cunningham

There is a certain kind of story that the Italians call *ben trovato* — that is, a story which, if not true, ought to be. A young man once consulted the late Karl Rahner, telling the great theologian that he had lost his faith and wanted advice about what he should read of Rahner's writings to regain that faith. Rahner told him not to read books but to join a group that serves the poor. That anecdote may well be *ben trovato,* but it contains a profound truth that has always sustained me in the church. Rahner's intuition was that those who "perform" the Gospel are those who provide the strongest apologetic for the faith.

Anyone who has studied church history or even read newspapers on a regular basis understands that there are many reasons to make one despair of one's membership in the church. Why put up with the evasions of a hierarchy that, in effect, condemned children to the horrors of repeated sexual abuse? Why be supine in the face of condemnations directed at certain people who are then effectively pushed away from receiving the Eucharist? Does not the resistance to contraception condemn some people to the risk of AIDS or unwanted pregnancies that tempt people to abortion? How often does a demand for "fidelity" actually mask a desire for the exercise of power? How many just drift away because of indifferent liturgies, pathetic homilies, or the anonymity of large parishes? One could lengthen out these examples but, in effect, whether the list is long or short it does drive many good people from the church. Who knows what varieties of reasons impel Catholics to become ex-Catholics? In this country alone it is estimated that there are more non-practicing Catholics than there are practicing Southern Baptists.

As one who is both a Catholic and professionally interested in Catholicism, I am more aware of these problems than are most people. Men and women I meet casually will unburden themselves with stories of unhappiness with the church that are beyond sad; who hurt because they reflect experience. For all this, however, I have never lost faith in the church and have never found even the imaginative power of being anything else than a Catholic. Like the fictional doctor Thomas More in Walker Percy's novel *Love in the Ruins,* I believe the whole thing from the Nicene Creed to papal infallibility, but always have problems with firm purpose of amendment.

To be a Catholic at a level beyond mere membership, however, demands that one look out for those signs of hope that are found within the church and give it cred-ibility. To me the place to look for those signs are not at the macro level of what this Vatican official says or that expert opines but at places closer to home. If one were to place a compass point at my street on a map and draw a circle to represent only three miles, what would one find? Well, the university where I teach, which has, not to put too fine a point on it, a certain Catholic *gravitas,* but also a Catholic Worker house, a center for the homeless that does more than provide "three hots and a cot," a shelter for abused women and their children, a house that provides day care for high-maintenance persons (the mentally or physically handicapped, Alzheimer's patients, etc.) so their care givers can have a day off, a health clinic for the poor sponsored by the local Catholic hospital, and a large St. Vincent de Paul Center and store.

Were one to examine those places closely one would see that they all drew upon some strand of the Catholic tradition, such as hospitals and homeless shelters, which can be traced back to the fourth century. When one magnifies and connects living Catholic places by the number of similar ones all over the world, one conjures up a huge skein of goodness that covers the planet. Most of these enterprises are noticed only by locals who appreciate their work, but when thought of as a whole, these constitute a true representation of the Catholic world.

Such centers of goodness and love are not peripheral to the "real" church. As Pope Benedict XVI recently wrote in his first encyclical (*Deus Caritas Est*), the church rests on three foundational activities: proclamation and witness to the Word (*kerygma/marturia*); sacramental worship (*leiturgia*); and loving service to others (*diakonia*). These three activities not only interpenetrate but also are mutually foundational.

If we are to understand why Catholicism still incarnates the work of Christ, we should do so not by looking for it only in the grand gesture — the papal trips, world youth days, eucharistic congresses, etc. — but in those eruptions of small incarnations of Christian community that radiate out from inspirations fed from the Great Tradition — responsive to and nourished by the local imperative to live out the gospel. What gives me trust in the church is to visit the small contemplative communities whose prayer lifts up the needs of humanity, the religious and laypeople who live in socially inhospitable places to preach the gospel both by word and deed.

Blessed John XXIII once likened the church to a fountain in the piazza — a source of water that cleanses and satisfies the whole village. The image is particularly potent because it calls attention to something primordial (water) available at some local place (the village). It is at this level of the church that we can find those images of hope that beckon us forward. We need to see them precisely as local and at the same time rooted as in something larger and older: the living water of the apostolic tradition. That is the primordial meaning of "catholic" that St. Ignatius of Antioch coined early in the second century — the entire body of believers, as opposed to the local community. It has always struck me that the bumper-sticker slogan of the ecology movement is equally, and perhaps more truly, applicable to Catholicism: think globally, act locally.

There is a final point. The cliché would have it that Catholicism is monolithic. In fact, the Catholic Church is unified by a common faith, common sacraments, and the unity of all local churches with the church of Peter (according to the *Catechism of the Catholic Church*), but beyond that, the faith offers a range of routes by which to follow the Way of Christ: diverse schools of spirituality, varied devotional practices, and communities within Community.

The Second Vatican Council, famously, gave us a vision of the church as the Pilgrim People of God. It is a stunning image because the nature of a pilgrimage is to have a destination but to always be on the Way. We strain forward and as with the paradigmatic pilgrims once described by Geoffrey Chaucer, we comprise a diverse community of saints, sinners, and all degrees in between. We are on the way, and I, for one, am satisfied to have my modest part of it.

～ 15 ～

Day by Day
Don Wycliff

I was brimming over with it when I graduated from college in 1969.

I was bereft of it after my wife announced two years ago that she wanted to be divorced.

I was intoxicated on it when each of my two sons was born.

I miss it most when I go home in the evening to an empty dwelling.

It's the one thing that I would give to my boys if I could give them only one thing.

It's what I often fear I'll never feel again.

Faith. Hope. Love. The three theological virtues.

"Have Faith, Hope, and Charity," Perry Como sang back in the 1950s. "That's the way to live successfully."

Like orange juice or Ovaltine, they not only were good, but they were good for you.

Faith and love have always seemed pretty straightforward to me. Hope was the slippery one.

Faith was what blind Bartimaeus demonstrated when he came to Jesus and asked the teacher to cure his blindness.

Faith was what Abraham had when he picked up his household and, at the command of his God, schlepped off from Mesopotamia to Palestine, trusting that he would become the patriarch of a great nation in whom others would find blessing.

> *Hope always seemed to me like a manufacturer's warranty against a defective faith.*

Faith was what my parents had when, in 1954, they decamped from the east Texas town that had always been home and took themselves and the first five of their eventual nine children to eastern Kentucky, depending on the kindness of strangers to help them make the better life that they sought.

And love — or charity, as Perry Como had it?

Charity was what Mother showed when she would fix a plate of bacon and eggs for one of the hoboes who knocked on our door from time to time.

Love was what Jesus was all about with his painful death on the cross — although at times it was hard to focus on Jesus' love amid the priests' grisly descriptions of his suffering and death. (The part that always got me was the crowning with thorns. Was the pain that Jesus felt then anything like the migraine pain I felt? If it was, then he *really* suffered.)

Love was what I felt for that beautiful dark-haired, dark-eyed classmate whom I and all the other boys were crazy about in fifth, sixth, and seventh grades. Something in my loins told me that this was love, but it most certainly was not charity.

But hope? Where did it fit in?

Hope always seemed to me like a manufacturer's warranty against a defective faith. It was a reserve parachute, a gallon of gas tucked away in the trunk of the car on the highway to heaven. If your faith was strong and resilient and, above all, *right,* why did you need hope?

I still don't know that I've figured it all out, but the last two years, in which I have seen my marriage and most of the routines of my life dissolve, have helped me begin to understand it.

Hope, I think, is our hedge against meaninglessness, against what the existentialists called absurdity, against the mocking laughter that overtakes you when the carefully built edifice of your life comes crashing down.

Hope is the faculty that lets us transmute tiny quantities of graciousness or optimism or kindness into enough fuel to get through the next day. And if you string enough days together, eventually you have the beginnings of a new life, a new (or renewed) faith, a new reason to keep living.

This is the stage at which I find myself now. I hope my way through the days. One, and then another, and then another....

Recently I felt for several days like Tom Sawyer listening in secretly on his own funeral. I had spent fifteen and a half years working at the *Chicago Tribune,* the last five and a half of those in something of a running public dialogue with readers as the newspaper's public editor. When news of my impending departure was published, a most amazing thing happened. By the dozens, and ultimately by the hundreds, people wrote and expressed appreciation for my work. This was one of my favorites:

Dear Mr. Wycliff,

Just a few words of appreciation for your column which I have enjoyed over the years. Thank you!

Yes, thank you for teaching me how to put words together so perfectly to explain a thought or idea. Thank you for the patience when you clarify an event or circumstances.

Oftimes, I thought it would be really great having you for a neighbor — perhaps conversing over the fence in the back yard.

Anyhow, now you are moving on. So, best wishes for continued success and may you be blessed with the best of health in the days ahead.

Sincerely,

Robert A. Ladewig

It's the part about having me as a neighbor that I particularly liked, because that's the tone I always tried to strike in my column.

Every writer hopes that he or she can touch someone in that fashion. Thank you, Mr. Ladewig, for letting me know that I did not hope in vain.

∼ 16 ∽

Hearts Close to Cracking
Mike Heher

Something can be learned about the nature of hope, I believe, by considering the odd but not so unusual experience of Elijah the prophet.

It started on what turned out to be the most decisive day in his campaign to demonstrate the power of Yahweh and the impotence of Ba'al. The odds were against him — 450 prophets of Ba'al to one prophet of Yahweh — but he was so confident that he had water poured over his sacrifice until it flowed down into the trench surrounding the altar. All day the prophets of Ba'al prayed, and so did Elijah, though he also spent a fair amount of time taunting his opponents. At sunset, as Elijah had expected, a fire like a thunderbolt came down from heaven that utterly consumed his wet offering and the wet wood beneath it as well as the wet stones and the muddy dust; it even "licked up the water that was in the trench" (1 Kings. 18:38). He who had been persecuted as "the troubler of Israel" had out Jezebeled Queen Jezebel. After so decisive a sign, he took his spoils by personally slaughtering all the prophets of Ba'al at the brook Kishon.

After the experience of that day, Elijah should have felt empowered to continue his provocative campaign without ambiguity or doubt. He was Yahweh's prophet; everyone had seen the signs. When, not long afterward, Elijah foresaw the end of a devastating drought, even Jezebel's husband, King Ahab, was impressed. Such affirmation should have led to an enlargement of Elijah's spirit; he should have been more hopeful than ever about his prophetic life and ministry. He wasn't.

I suspect it was because the battle was personal; Elijah wanted Jezebel to acknowledge that there was no God but Yahweh. She didn't, and he was soon on the run from her murderous wrath. Elijah went to Beer-sheba, which was as far south as he could go and remain in Israelite territory. Then he went farther, walking a day into the wilderness, leaving behind even his servant. Literally "in extremis," Elijah savored no sweetness. He did not feel elect. Confessing that he was no better than his ancestors before him, he lay down in the shade of the only tree around and fell asleep, begging God to be allowed to die. True, he may have preferred to die in the wilderness by Yahweh's hand — another sort of sacrifice — than to submit to martyrdom in Jezebel's clutches. But I don't think that explains it.

What happened to him? What initiated this crisis of confidence and this exhaustion of spirit, this pitiless disillusionment? Had he realized that his dramatic demonstration had reduced Yahweh to Ba'al's level, to nothing more than a more powerful rival? Or was he brought up short by the realization that *he* should have been the one at Yahweh's beck and call, and not vice versa?

On these questions the Bible is silent, but I have come to believe that Elijah suffered what James Alison has called "a heart-close-to-cracking," an unexpected mixture of inner confusion, listlessness, and compunction. Elijah's notion of himself and God had become unglued. What he thought their relationship was, was no more, or perhaps never was. And there was for Elijah quite literally no way back. One could argue that Elijah was being punished for his arrogant abuse of divine power, but I think he simply found himself in a place many of us find ourselves in at times, a kind of purgatory where we suddenly are able to see, to borrow from Flannery O'Connor, in our own "shocked and altered faces" that even our "virtues were being burned away."

We notice that the bluster has gone out of our rhetoric, and we ourselves no longer believe what we are saying. At the end of our protests and letter-writing campaigns and demonstrations, we are beat. We have spent ourselves "working the system" without achieving the results for which we have striven. Or we have been able to do something obvious and impressive, as did Elijah, but we doubt our success will have any useful effect on the seemingly impenetrable world of woe.

It is a time when we have come to the end of our fervent prayers, our devout religious practices, our impassioned hymns, and undoubting rosaries. Perhaps we have even come to the end of our never-fail novenas, our scapulars and medals, our expectation of miracles at Chimayo and Lourdes and Tepeyac. As with Elijah, the heart comes close to cracking because we have not been able to do what we had hoped, perhaps even promised to do, and our prayers have not been efficacious. Our situation appears hopeless.

But Elijah's story then took an unexpected turn. He was awakened twice by an angel who told him to eat the sun-baked cakes before him and get up and go to the mountain of God. With that sustenance and guidance, Elijah was able to make an exhaustive pilgrimage of forty days and forty nights. (I imagine he had some leftover cakes to nibble along the way.)

This story is not about Elijah's perseverance, for he did not pull himself up by his own sandal straps. Rather, he was helped. Hope is always "relative to the idea of help," writes William Lynch, S.J., in *Images of Hope: Imagination as Healer of the Hopeless* (Notre Dame, 1965), a book he wrote while living in residence among the mentally ill. Hope, he said, "depends. It looks to the outside world." Hope was exactly what Elijah couldn't give himself. He received it as a gift in the form of a messenger, a companion, a cook. By the end of his pilgrimage, Elijah no longer needed to depend on the fury of the great strong wind, or the unhinging earthquake, or the avenging thunderbolt of fire; he was able to recognize Yahweh in "a still small voice," no more than something whispered, perhaps just an indecipherable murmur (see 1 Kings 19:12).

In American spirituality, both Protestant and Catholic, there is a preference for the virtue of the individual. Jesus is *my* personal Lord and Savior. We sit as Quakers, each awaiting our own personal inspirations. We pray our rosary beads on the way to work and call on our chosen patron saints. We do not like our preachers to tell us how to vote or what to think. All we will tolerate is a certain level of inspiration, just enough uplift to keep us going on our own. We much prefer the virtue of individual perseverance to the hope that comes as a gift from God.

Perhaps this is why we are so surprised and uncomfortable when we find ourselves poor in spirit. When we are mournful or meek, we tell ourselves to snap out of it. We are aggrieved under the yoke of persecution, more likely to sue our oppressors than forgive them. When we have done all we have been commanded, when we say, "We are unprofitable servants; we have done what we were obliged to do" (Luke 18:10), we are not delighted at this state of affairs; we would prefer to have done it all ourselves and received a pat on the back from God. We hate being dependent.

This may explain our clamorous desire to get past our current crises. Let us rebuild our shaken institutions, and quickly, and reassert ourselves as God's people. Let us be known again, we tell ourselves, as Yahweh's worthy and chosen and strong — those who can make things happen.

But what if, however weakly, we remained where we are with hearts still close to cracking? What if we wait, veiled and hidden from the world, continuing our modest but helpful tasks, watching not for fire or quake or wind but for the experience of God that comes to us as a "still small voice"? What might we receive? An unexpected joyfulness? Is this not what Cleopas and his companion learned on the road to Emmaus and in the breaking of the bread? The scandal of Jesus' incarnation is his *kenosis*. He poured himself out. He was, as can be seen in the Gospels, quite careful that his signs and wonders were not interpreted as acts of power but expressions of love and mercy.

Might we begrudgingly imagine for ourselves a mission less focused on proving ourselves and more on finding, joining, freeing, and protecting other delicate, cracking hearts? Might we find the joyfulness of a Charles de Foucauld, a kind of recluse who, like Elijah, also had trouble discerning God's will for himself, but who possessed a nomad's passion for offering hospitality? Might our chastened institutions become needed refuges in a world that seems utterly mad for religious ascendancy, even to the point of violence?

Hearts that have come close to cracking are skittish, like crabs without shells, prone to suspicions and bouts of cynicism, perhaps too careful. What saves and protects them is solidarity, an unexpected circle of angels: messengers, companions, cooks. It is a gift as welcome and as human as an evening barbecue where children splash and squeal while relatives and friends drift in and out of each other's conversations. They express opinions, ask questions, and tell stories, or often enough, retell them for the pleasure of the telling and hearing. Gradually, in the kitchen or at the grill, while watching the children play and sipping another beer in the shade, the adults shift their conversation to what is most precious and close, in moments when, as Cardinal Newman's motto so wonderfully claimed, "heart speaks to heart." The sun is setting and candles are lit. Everyone gathers around the table of food, for we are all ravenous and will remain ever so this side of heaven. We eat together and our hearts are not cracking, not tonight; no, they are burning within us.

∼ 17 ∽

Faces

Paul Wilkes

I am a journalist and have written about Catholicism and Catholic issues for many years, so on occasion I am asked to speak before church groups and diocesan convocations. While some of the larger, more public gatherings have brought memorable moments, it is when I conduct parish missions that I inevitably feel humbled and awestruck by what I see in the faces of the people in the assembly.

In one way or another, my mission theme invariably revolves around a simple idea: not letting anything get in the way of a full Catholic life. There is a richness and potency to our faith that we sometimes miss appreciating if we wallow in guilt, inadequacies, or legalities. I use a simple ritual on the first night to try to point out that God awaits us, just as we are. I have the church darkened and a single candle lit on the altar. I ask the people to come forward. Here on the bare altar, I tell them, they can lay their burdens down. Here they can ask for whatever they need. Here they can speak intimately to a friend.

If you could be with me as I sit off to the side and watch the slowly moving line of men and women approach the altar, you would see what I see: hope in those faces.

> *Hope is alive in parishes and parishioners today sometimes in spite of what happens in the larger church.*

Joe and Mary Catholic in our parishes have been through rough times in their own lives and the life of their church. Life has buffeted them, disappointed them, troubled them. Faith has sometimes had a hollow, distant ring. Their church has sometimes been insensitive to them, sometimes untrustworthy, sometimes deaf to their cries. Children, family, and friends have said "enough" and are no longer practicing Catholics. All this hurts, and hurts deeply.

But as they approach the altar, their purity of heart is almost palpable. I imagine there are saints and sinners, believers and doubters, among them, but such arbitrary barriers crumble as their darkened faces first become visible, then lighten as they come into the glow emanating from the altar. They are coming to the One who, after all, knows them so well, from whom no secrets are hid. I can see tears streaming down some faces; I see expectant eyes and eyes cast down. No matter, the light is there for them all.

It is in the parish that I see hope most alive in our church. As a journalist, I have covered Vatican events and bishops' conferences, but somehow I never feel as close to hope in those places as I do when I am among so-called ordinary Catholics in a parish. The parish is where Catholicism comes alive. We may be part of a great parish or one less than dynamic, but the parish is our spiritual home nonetheless, a place of community unlike any other in our lives.

Hope is alive in parishes and parishioners today sometimes in spite of what happens in the larger church. Catholics are quite tolerant of those in their midst who have been divorced, had an abortion, are gay or have, as we used to say, "fallen away." They know how hard it is to live a righteous life today, but in the parish, when they gather, they find the hope that they can make a difference in the world, that God will show them a way, that their next act is going to be Christ-like.

And Christ himself, we should remember, needed a community to nourish his hope that others would come to understand the ways of a Loving Father. He needed the first parishioners so that loneliness or despair or fatigue would not prevail. It is this "light of Christ" that is reflected in those faces.

But as in the time of Christ, so today: the uber-righteous tell people of hope that their belief is not proper or sufficient or deep enough. Some — in positions of authority or self-appointed — stand between the candle and the people, not allowing its glow, its warmth, to be experienced. They forget that Christ came to bring tender mercy, not inflict harsh judgment. For them, judgment is all, the way is narrow, the rubrics of Catholicism more important than the spirit of Catholicism: the promise of Christ's generosity.

In this time when our church sometimes seems more interested in closing doors than opening them, of extinguishing the flame of hope rather than letting it shine forth, I look back to good Pope John XXIII for inspiration. At the beginning of the Vatican Council that he called into being — with so much hope in his own heart — John XXIII pronounced that he would not listen to the "prophets of doom," who saw nothing but corruption and sin in the modern world. He saw goodness where all they could see was evil; hope where they felt despair. In the spirit of this great apostle of hope, the council cast a new vision of what it is to be Catholic. Catholics could now approach Christ and his altar with the renewed confidence that they were not in the presence of some unappeasable celestial scorekeeper, but of a companion who could listen and understand, who stood ready to assist and strengthen.

There is so much goodness in our parishes that I sometimes find myself overwhelmed as I complete a parish mission. On the final night, before the people depart, a single candle once again burns on the altar in a darkened church. That tiny flame is then spread from parishioner to parishioner, from hand-held candle to hand-held candle. There is hope in those illuminated faces, the reflected light of Christ. And I hope that even as these men and women extinguish the flame at the door of the sanctuary, each of them will continue to glow in their own way. The flame is within them.

～ 18 ～

The Crossroad
Phyllis Zagano

The ladies by the roadside smiled. They were genuinely happy. The sun shone on their toothless faces as they held up bags of water for us to buy there, at the crossroad of El Rosario de la Paz. Across the bend in the road another woman cooked on an outdoor grill, the sort you see at carnivals in small towns along equally dusty roads. Except this was her kitchen, and the lean-to behind was her house, where small ones scampered about, peeking out from behind cardboard walls at the tall strange pale women, that May morning in El Salvador.

I often come back to that day, that crossroad. We turned left, leaving the road from Hacienda San Francisco, and ended up in front of where those women lived. The other way, straight ahead, led to the police barracks where Ita Ford and her companions were first taken on December 2, 1980, before their hijacked van sped back across the "T" in the road the other way, to Hacienda San

118

Francisco, and to their deaths. Four Americans, dead and buried at the side of a dusty road.

The who, the what, the why, will never be quite answered. The facts are overgrown now, by weeds of fading memories. The four were surely killed by Salvadoran troops — National Guardsmen — on orders from a higher authority. But the facts make no sense, no sense at all.

We do not know what goes on in the deepest recesses of strangers' hearts. When people we know of do something stupid we ask, "What were they thinking?" This is darker, but stupid all the same. What were they thinking?

We look at this one incident, now twenty-seven years old, and see how despair can both cause and be caused by the vilest acts. Those men, those five or six young gun-toting men, those trigger-happy Salvadoran soldiers placed their hope in this one act, this common violent braggadocio of small and stupid people.

Perhaps the senior officer at the police barracks said "go away," "get rid of them," "this is stupid." And so that is what they did. They went away and they got rid of them, and it was very stupid.

Where is the hope? Where is the hope that somehow something somewhere will make sense? Where is the hope that brings out light from deranged belief in evil?

Is this brutal act any different now than it was twenty-seven years ago? It most certainly is not for the people who lost them, the people named Ford and Clark and Donovan and Kazel. They suffer daily the knowledge that the narrowing dirt road was the last the women saw, the rumbling van was the last they knew, the anger and the spitting and the molestations were the last they felt until the hard cold end of the barrel of a gun pressed against their necks and heads, and there was nothing left to see or know or feel.

Hope is something difficult to talk of in these times, and hope was something difficult to talk of in those times as well. There was no common decency, no respect for those who cared about the poor.

Where is the hope that brings out light from deranged belief in evil?

Today it is the same. The structures that we know and love keep crumbling all around us. The first we heard of these four women's deaths was in a tiny newspaper story. Every day it seems another four hundred words whisper another murder, another atrocity, another tragedy. Behind those words is an ocean of despairing fact. Where do we place our hope?

What is hope anyway? It is much more than simply not despairing, although it is very much not despairing and continually and affirmatively not despairing. It is refusing to believe that the acts we cannot control affect our fate, but it is also refusing to believe that the quietist response is what we need. We can do something, we must do something, but the first something we should do is hope.

Hope, as a theological virtue, involves trust. It is the basic understanding of who and how God made the world and us, and that God cares for all creation in a deeply personal way. But fewer people place their hope in God. Fewer people trust God at all.

Five or six stupid men with guns trusted their brute strength and their connections to a government as corrupt as ever known. Their trust, for whatever it was they hoped in, brought them to the brink of despair and left them there. They thought that they were heroes. They thought they would be praised. Instead they slunk in hiding in a cover-up until at last their sins saw the light of day.

Four American women hoped as well. They trusted the goodness of the people of Salvador, and their families did too. They hoped that there could be an end to war and dirt and poverty. They hoped that someone somewhere soon would feed the starving children, would find the disappeared, would quiet midnight gunfire. But most of all they hoped in God.

The collision that dark night along the road from El Rosario de la Paz to Hacienda San Francisco was between light and dark, between the innocent and the guilty, between hope and despair.

It is the same daily collision that slides beneath every bad decision, the one that helps the pastor pocket cash, or helps the bishop cover up. It is the same daily collision that sometimes brings about a win for faith or hope or charity.

No matter whether it is simple missioners or corrupt guardsmen, no matter whether poor parishioners or important churchmen, the collisions are all the same, and the motivations are as well.

The consequences depend on where you place your trust, on where you place your hope.

❧ 19 ❧

Hope in the Ruins
Colleen Carroll Campbell

My father has always been a man of hope. Thanks to his natural Irish optimism, Dad spent much of his career in motion, moving my mother, brother, and me to a half-dozen states where better opportunities beckoned and God's call seemed to lead.

Seen through Dad's eyes, every new city was bursting with adventures. Even our problems were pregnant with promise. Whether consoling my weepy six-year-old teammates after our first T-ball loss, coaxing me through an awkward transition to junior high school, or supporting me when I decided to break up with a college sweetheart, Dad always reminded me that hope and suffering were intertwined, and hope had the last word. "Remember," he would tell me, quoting St. Paul's letter to the Romans, "everything works together for good for those who love God."

I believed because I knew that Dad believed. His faith in God's providence shaped every decision he made, from his choice to leave the higher pay and prestige of an executive job and direct diocesan family life programs for the church, to his peaceful resolve about putting his family's needs ahead of his own desires day after day, year after year.

Dad's trust in God was the fruit of prayer. I learned this as a girl, when I would rise before dawn and find Dad in his office, reading his breviary or praying in silence. Spotting me in the doorway, he would grin and wave me inside. I would scurry toward him, hop on his lap with a mangled baby doll in tow, and pour out my hopes and dreams, nightmares and worries. He would listen, then tell me about the heavenly Father I could trust to care for all my needs.

As the years passed, my problems changed, but Dad's advice never did. It was always grounded in hope, a hope anchored not in happy circumstances but in the promise that God never abandons us. Consumed by the chaotic busyness of collegiate life, I would find eloquent letters from Dad in my dormitory mailbox that urged me to make time for prayer, discern God's will in my decisions, and tap into the rich wisdom of Scripture each day. "God's revelation is found there," he wrote during my sophomore year, when I was wrestling with a choice of majors, "tailored to your personal needs, questions, and hopes."

At the time I read those words, I was too harried to fully digest Dad's advice. He seemed far away, too old and placid to understand the pressures of my young life. But his words would return to me just a few years later, as I watched him struggle through the most difficult journey of his life. It was in Dad's crucible of dementia that I came to see what his hope was made of; it was there that I learned why he had refused to hope in anything less than the promise of eternal life in Jesus Christ.

The Alzheimer's diagnosis came on a bleak January day in 1996, during my last semester of college. I remember gripping the telephone and staring at the bare white walls of my bedroom as I absorbed the shock of my mother's words, my eyes falling on the Celtic cross that Dad had brought me from Ireland a few months earlier. I wanted to believe the promise it symbolized, to cling to the hope I heard in Dad's voice when he told me, "Everything will work out." But I felt only numbness, then emptiness and dread.

In the next few years, I managed to focus on my career more than Dad's decline. But as his condition deteriorated, his suffering became harder to ignore. Shortly after the diagnosis, Dad lost his last job — a pastoral care position at a local hospital where he was beloved by the patients but could no longer find their rooms. Now retired, he was losing himself piece by piece: his friends, his freedom, his memories, his mind.

Yet Dad's hope remained steadfast. Walking into my parents' home, I would find him reading his breviary or children's books about the saints (he could no longer comprehend the Carmelite treatises on mystical prayer that he once loved) and reciting his rosary. He would clap his hands upon seeing me, clasp me in a bear hug, then lean forward to confide what he had pondered that day. "I have something important to tell you," he would say. "We can trust God. We're in good shape."

At the adult day care center Dad attended, I would find him making the rounds, singing "When Irish Eyes Are Smiling" and consoling fellow dementia patients who writhed in rage and confusion. "We're all in God's hands," he would say, as he stroked their arms. "We'll be okay."

By January 2006, Dad had lost the ability to dress and bathe himself and he required help with eating and toileting. My mother had lovingly cared for him at home for a decade, but when her first-choice nursing home finally found a place for him after a four-year wait, she moved him there.

The transition has been difficult. Paired with a noisy roommate and a constantly changing cast of nurses and aides, Dad has struggled to adjust. He is too disoriented to know that he no longer lives at home — my mother's lengthy daily visits seem to have convinced him that they still live together — but he knows when the person bathing or dressing or toileting him is not his wife. He clearly experiences moments of loneliness, fear, and confusion. Sometimes I find him sitting at the nurses' station, waving and attempting to chat with aides who pass him in silence. One day my mother found him alone in the dining room, holding his head in his hands and pleading to Pope John Paul II to send help from heaven. "I was confused and frightened," he told me a few minutes later. "I didn't know what was going on."

The suffering Dad has endured — from the first terrifying days of his diagnosis, when he knew what lay before him, to this late stage of his disease, when he cannot comprehend the world around him and must rely on strangers for his most basic needs — has challenged my easy ideas about hope. Hope based on a sunny disposition or happy circumstances or the promise of better times ahead cannot stand in the face of Alzheimer's. Dad's optimism cannot protect him from the agitation of dementia. And his condition will not improve.

The only hope he has that can withstand this disease is the authentic Christian hope that sustained my father all his life, the hope that he once tried to teach me through words but ultimately taught by example. It is the hope described in the eighth chapter of Romans that Dad loved so much: "I consider that the sufferings of this present time are as nothing compared with the glory to be revealed for us.... For in hope we were saved. Now hope that sees for itself is not hope. For who hopes for what one sees? But if we hope for what we do not see, we wait with endurance."

With endurance my father has waited — through the early frustration of memory loss, through the later fog of confusion, through the final humiliation of total dependence. His hope has grown more luminous with each passing year, refined by suffering and undimmed by dementia. It has radiated outward to friends and strangers, caregivers and fellow patients.

Even now, my father spreads hope. In his nursing home, Dad ministers to the elderly nuns who stare blankly from their wheelchairs. He provokes smiles with his courtly bows and tips of an imaginary hat. "Great to see you," he'll say, as he saunters the halls. "You're the best." Led into a room full of dementia patients, he will find his way to the corner where the most distressed one among them is muttering incoherently. Plopping himself down next to her, he will sing "Danny Boy" until she grows quiet and calm. "I like to take care of people," he will tell me, when he can remember what he has just done.

The staff has come to know Dad as the chipper Irishman, forever meeting and greeting. Some of the adult children of other residents have also discovered his charms. One searches for Dad after a rough day at the office; another plays catch with Dad in the hallway and howls at his one-liners. "We needed him around this place," she told me once. "We really needed him."

I need him, too. Duty often leads me to his doorstep, but love makes me stay. Finding him reading his breviary, or singing to strangers, or bowing his head at Mass reminds me that there truly is a love stronger than death, stronger even than dementia. It is the love I see in Dad's eyes after he receives Jesus in the Eucharist, when he does not know I am watching. I follow his gaze to the massive crucifix that hangs above the altar in his nursing home chapel. Dad fixes his eyes on it, slowly raising his right hand and pointing to the figure of Jesus. Then he points back to himself, keeping his eyes locked on Jesus and nodding as if to say, *Yes, I still believe.*

This is my father's thanksgiving, the hope to which he clings. It is the one thing necessary upon which he staked his entire life. And it will never be taken from him.

20

Miracle
Cullen Murphy

"Do you believe in miracles?"

It's a question I've heard all my life — one that I can recall asking others at a very young age, and one that I've been asked in turn at a considerably older age. The question is complicated, as even youngsters understand. What, first of all, do you mean by the term itself — "miracle"? And then, what do you mean by "believe in"? And so the question "Do you believe in miracles?" tags along like a shadow, impossible to grasp and impossible to escape.

But every so often something happens that affords a glimpse of an answer — a glimpse also into the very idea of hope as an escarpment beyond the realm of mere coincidence, where willful actions by flesh-and-blood people lead to something that looks to me like grace.

I'll tell the story as I remember it being told to me. A young woman friend of mine some years ago was suffering from a serious neurological disorder of unknown nature. She has since recovered. But one day during the period of her illness, while riding on the subway in New York City, she suddenly experienced the loss of her eyesight. She waited a few moments, thinking her vision might return, but it did not. And so she did what anyone might do, though it required a certain amount of trust in humankind. She turned to the person next to her, explained what had happened, and asked if this person, who turned out to be a woman, could serve as a guide up to street level. The woman heard out my friend, took her by the arm, and said, "Of course."

The train came to a stop. The doors slid open. My friend held tight to the woman as she left the subway car and threaded her way along the crowded platform. They negotiated the turnstile, and once beyond the two of them flowed with the traffic toward the steps leading up to the outer world. As they began to climb the steps, my friend's sight slowly began to return — the light at the top coming into view, the jostling people all around turning slowly into visible shapes. My friend turned to the woman at her elbow, who had led her from the subway car, and saw that the woman's other hand held a thin white cane, and that she was blind.

I'm not sure I'll ever know the right name for this event. But I think of it always when I try to locate hope. Because so often it turns out to be at the miraculous intersection of one person's faith and another's charity.

❦ 21 ❦

The Longing

A. G. Harmon

My image of hope has most often been an innocent one, distinguished from other virtues only by the physical attitude of Jesus in the depictions of the rosary. Hope, the virtue memorialized on Ascension Day, is represented by the Lord rising to the heavens, his gaze upward, with the astonished apostles at some distance below the divine, dangling feet. For a long time this has satisfied me, as it is different from the immediately preceding representation of faith, in which Jesus emerges from his shattered tomb in white-robed glory. The big difference lay in the fact that in the former, Jesus is flying — in the latter, standing resolutely still.

But if pressed to put my images aside — either by my own inquisitiveness or that of others — I have had more trouble with hope's proper definition. I know its meaning on some intuitive level, and have both practiced and sinned against it. But when asked to draw clear parameters about it, the task has proved difficult. The term is employed so blithely, so cavalierly, that its very use can contribute to its obscurity. In the end, I am left with finding hope's meaning by first defining what it is not, and what I suspect that I and others have generally confused it with.

First, hope is not faith, for which it is easily mistaken. It is not belief. It is not acknowledgment or assent to the reality of that which we cannot see. We often interchange the two terms when we speak: "It's one of my hopes," we say, when we really mean it is one of the things we believe in, or "I have faith it will work out," when we mean that we hope it will. Perhaps the error lies in the fact that faith is a necessary precursor to hope. Augustine asked what can be hoped for that is not first believed, and so hope follows from faith, as naturally as the expectation of slaked thirst follows from the belief that we have found water. It seems right to say that hope is one of the things that faith brings us — that we must believe in hope, just as we must believe in other truths of Christian conviction. (And must we first love, before we can believe or hope? It is an interesting question, better answered elsewhere and by others.) But hope is not itself belief, the core and cache of tenets to which we conform our lives.

Neither is hope optimism, as Bruce Marshall has cautioned against our concluding. It is not a positive outlook, an unflagging assurance that things will resolve themselves in a way to our liking. This, it seems, is what most people have in mind when they speak of hope. I have most often considered it a kind of doggedness, a marathon of smiling-through-gritted-teeth determination. Optimism, when seen rightly, is a stance toward events, a means of mental preparedness that keeps us answering the bell when it rings. While it has its place, it can also be misguided, starry-eyed, and even blind when there is no solid reason for it, leading to painful frustration when things fall through. But again, hope is not an outlook; hope cannot disappoint. It is only a manner of speaking when we tell the doctor not to give us "false hope," as such a construction is actually an oxymoron. What we really mean by that formulation is: "Don't lie to me. Don't tell me there is something to be optimistic about when there is not." The Christian virtue of hope, on the other hand, has as its object that which cannot be false.

Finally, hope is not fulfillment itself. By its nature, hope is longing, yearning, desiring. Hope may meet fulfillment, but when it does so, it ceases to be hope. We cannot hope for what we already have. With this understanding we avoid another possible mistake. Hope is not static, but active. While it is true that we hope for *things,* and so we each have our "hopes," there is less of the noun in this term than the verb. Those hopes are the objects of our desires — we are "hoping," always "hoping" for those "hopes," and the progressive form comes closest to capturing the essence of constant striving.

This appreciation of hope's true nature — its dynamism, its longing — helps us understand its role in our lives. Hope is literally the energy within, that which sustains us on a passage that would be too arduous and dispiriting otherwise. The joy hope brings is in anticipation of the good that will flow from its object. But in this truth lies that which is most difficult in its meaning. What is the proper object of hope? What are we right to hope for?

For the Catholic, the right object of hope is God, to trust that he is who he said he is, and will do what he says he will do. This must be managed carefully, however, because hope cannot be divested of its power by turning it into a vague, forbidding cloud, so general in meaning that it forbids the senses. This would make hope a mere truism, safe because it is ineffective, with God at the border of heaven, turned the other way. Catholics must believe in the God the church witnesses to, and hope in his manifestation in our lives through the things that are consistent with the good. Hope is practical in this way, even pragmatic, in that it is looking for the effects of faith and expecting them to come to be. What we hope for is a God who is concerned for us now, as we live in this world and prepare for the next. We may even hope for that good to manifest a certain way, though this must be approached with openness and humility. We simply must not presume that we know exactly what that good is, or all that it is, for to do so would be to presume to know the definition of God. Rather, to hope rightly is to appreciate, as best we can, the vastness of the Christian promise, and to trust it is meant for us. In this way, hope is like a good view of a long valley, of the abundance of all that it holds, and the anticipation that somehow, some way, the good within is meant for us. That is what we must want; that is what we must be confident we will have.

~ 22 ~

Onward

Luke Timothy Johnson

Novelist Tony Hillerman entitled his admirable memoir *Seldom Disappointed*. The title came from the maxim delivered by his Irish-Catholic mother, a survivor of the Depression-era Oklahoma Dust Bowl: "Keep your expectations low, and you'll seldom be disappointed." In this pithy admonition, I recognized the truth of my own life and that of my five brothers and sisters. We also grew up in poverty, the children of a widow who herself died at forty-five. Losing our parents and all form of human security at an early age, we all became absolute fatalists. We expect nothing from life except suffering and loss. But I have never been among such jolly, life-affirming, hope-filled folk as my siblings.

This is, I have come to understand, not an unusual combination. On one side, we see people surrounded by privilege and possibility who cannot seem either to enjoy or employ their gifts. On the other side, we see extraordinary ebullience among contestants at the Special

Olympics and radiant joy among those for whom every breath is a victory of the will.

Here's what I have come to think about hope, the most elusive of human dispositions and Christian virtues. Hope is the mysterious sense of something or someone more beyond what we touch and see, that calls us beyond what we touch and see, and thereby enables us to engage what we touch and see without being defined or trapped by what we touch and see. Hope is the spark of freedom within us that we sense comes not from ourselves but another. It has little to do with hoping for something or hoping that something will happen. It has much to do with hoping in something or someone who, oddly enough, seems also to be hoping in us. We hope in the Living God even when we do not know it is the Living God in whom we hope.

The mystery of hope — the mysteriousness of hope — intrigues me more than ever at the age of sixty-three, when I am more sharply aware, not of limits that might be overcome by dint of effort, but of the apparently absolute limit to human expectation imposed by mortality. After years of strenuous parenthood and arduous scholarship and teaching, I am impressed most of all by the way in which mortality colors my sense of all human achievement — especially mine.

Thomas Aquinas was said to have declared at the time of his death that his magisterial theological works seemed just so much straw. I am beginning to see what he meant. Not that I have any accomplishment comparable to Aquinas's, but I have worked hard for many years, and now, as my body grows more tired and my memory grows more unreliable, my efforts also seem to have less punch and point.

All systems, including mine, it seems, tend toward entropy. I begin to suspect that the world leaves me even before I am ready to leave the world. My students, like my children, grow away from, rather than toward, me; they may enlarge the circle of my presence but at the cost of my presence.

> *Hope is the spark of freedom within us that we sense comes not from ourselves but another.*

I grow similarly detached from the academy and the church, the two institutions within which I have labored most of my life. I cannot grow too dismayed or excited at the appointment of a new dean or the election of a new pope. It does not seem likely that curricular reform or seminary reform will solve anything important or for long. Like all human structures, the academy struggles against the barbarism within its walls; like all bodies, the body of Christ that is the church experiences corruption.

Why, then, do I keep grading "C" papers even when they persist in being "C" papers? Why do I leap to receive calls from my children even though I know well that they may not be bringing good news? Why do my wife, Joy, and I savor the sweetness of each moment of life even as we feel life slipping away? Why does it gladden me to welcome converts to the church even when I know the trials that await them? I once thought that my positive disposition toward life was due to animal high spirits. But as the animal in me weakens, the spirit does not seem to waver. Perhaps my hope really is in something/someone other than myself.

As a teacher, I do not hope that all "C" students will turn into "A" students. Rather, I hope in the Living God who constantly, in every generation, sets fires in the minds of some of the young, igniting in them the drive and the desire to take up the never-ending battle for truth and beauty and goodness against the forces of barbarism even within themselves. So I cast little seeds of thought, hoping in my students and in the One who can gift them with wisdom. As a theologian who loves the church, I do not hope that ecclesiastical policy will suddenly perfectly realize God's will. Rather, I speak and write with hope in the living God who can, in every generation, raise up prophets from among us to carry out a powerful witness, not only to the world, but to the church as sacrament of the world.

As a father, I do not hope that my children will avoid all suffering and pain; rather I hope in them, and I hope in the Living God who can sustain them through all their suffering and pain. As a husband, I do not hope that Joy's body will suddenly become wholly healthy, but I hope in her, who has never ceased to hope even when her body has betrayed her, and I hope in the Living God, who draws Joy toward the true Life that is eternal. And as the one who walks with Joy toward that inevitable end, I hope in the Living God whose tender mercies might include a place for those who place their hope in him.

Part Three

BELIEVE

∽ 23 ∽

Uncommon Hope
Kenneth L. Woodward

I've reached that stage in life where it seems there are no more weddings or even baptisms to attend, only funerals. "Get used to it," my older sister tells me. Sometimes she attends three in one day. Friends die, and looking at their bodies, so unlike the ones you hugged or hailed with a slap on the back, you realize that whatever hopes they had in life have been realized — or not.

Contrary to the adage, hope does not spring eternal. "Abandon all hope, you who enter here," is the chilling message Dante sees etched over the portal to Hell. The hope referred to, of course, is the hope of eternal life with God, the hope that transcends all lesser hopes. It's the ultimate hope that counters ultimate despair, the hope the substance of which, St. Paul tells us, is faith. It is the only form of hope that really interests me now.

Years ago, when death was on my mind, but my own seemed impossibly remote, I asked my friend and some-times mentor Rabbi Abraham Heschel how he imagined

145

the afterlife. We were in his cramped study at the Jewish Theological Seminary, piles of books like stalagmites on the surface of his desk and teetering on shelves above him. (If ever the building shook, I often thought, he would be buried then and there with the things he loved the most.) His answer was as austere as it was direct: "I trust the God Who made me what I am to do with me what He will." Six months later, and all too soon, he was dead.

Hope, then, requires trust. "I go before you, to prepare a place for you," Jesus tells his uncomprehending disciples. In other words, "Trust me."

But Catholics also believe that the church is the body of Christ. Not a spiritual body of "true Christians" but an organic communion of saints and sinners that transcends time and space. "There's something you have to understand, Ken," Methodist theologian Albert Outler, a wise and gentle soul, once told me. It was just after the close of Vatican Council II, a time of great optimism for Catholics and of renewed hopes for unity among all Christians. "Deep down, we Protestants distrust the church structures we've created," he wanted me to know. "But for Catholics, I've noticed, even the most critical among them, 'Holy Mother the Church' is always 'HolyMothertheChurch.'"

What Outler meant is that Catholics assume that the church is simply there, and always will be, like the sun that also rises. This is the church that we are also asked to trust. Does it merit that trust?

We Catholics have been sorely tested by the child-abuse scandals involving not only predator priests but also the bishops who wrongly protected them. These scandals exposed a clerical mode of thinking and behaving that seems to resist rectification. But it is far from the worst crisis that ever hit the church — think of the times when "the year of three popes" meant three rival claimants to the papacy — and those who claim to be scandalized beyond reconciliation by the present scandal should study church history.

When I think of the church, I think of the various "communities of memory and hope" (the phrase comes from sociologist Robert Bellah) that have nurtured, formed, and sustained me throughout my life. They have at various times included parish priests, nuns who taught me, friends who supported me, professors who instructed me, colleagues who encouraged me, and above all the exceptional figures who showed me, by their example, how to be a better Catholic than, left to my own devices, I could ever be. Whenever I encounter people like this — and not all of them are Catholics — my hopes for the church are sustained. Trouble is, the sort of people I've been describing seem now in short supply.

Any source of hope for the church must be measured against the current temptations to despair. This is not the place or space to recount all the obvious ills that plague

American Catholics. But high on my own list is the astounding failure of the church to pass on the faith to its young. Second — and a function of the first — is the decline in vocations to the priesthood and the religious life. Third would be the irrational and crippling fear of lay initiative by members of the American hierarchy. And then there is the divisiveness — the sheer nastiness displayed by conservative and liberal Catholic elites toward each other.

The church should expect of Catholics uniformity of faith, not uniformity of thought. Its leaders should be pleased that lay elites have emerged and given voice to diverse strategies for renewal of the church and of society. Conservatives are right to stress the need for solid formation in the faith, wrong to suppose that this can be accomplished by creating a new Catholic subculture, much less by demanding their own version of "orthodoxy" as the test of true belief. Liberals are right to emphasize engagement with society and to reject a fundamentalist reliance on every word from Rome. But they are wrong when they suppose that expressions of the faith are infinitely pliable, or that secular strategies can substitute for the advance of what Jesus understood as God's kingdom.

If there is a source of hope in the present malaise, I suppose it's this: the wind of triumphalism has been sucked out of the church. The "Catholic moment" in

American public life disappeared almost as soon as it was announced. Humility is now the virtue of our necessity.

My hopes? They are for my children and grandchildren now, that they may find in the church the kinds of communal support that formed, uplifted, and challenged older Catholics like me. Indifference is what defies the Holy Spirit. The church is what Catholics themselves make of what's been given them; bishops merely own the store.

The hardest saying in the Gospels surely is "Not mine, but Your will be done." But it becomes easier as you watch the margins of your life retract, bit-by-bit. These days, I think of one old friend, Cardinal Joseph Bernardin. Told his cancer was terminal, he handed over the store to others and found a community of hope and memory among other cancer victims. Friends say he laughed a lot those last days despite the pain. Virgil discerned "the tears in things," but comedy comes naturally to those who learn to trust in the Lord.

Ultimately, not to hope is to not trust the Holy Spirit. We trust because we must — because, as Gerard Manley Hopkins came to understand, "the Holy Ghost over the bent / World broods with warm breast and with ah! bright wings." I believe that.

~ 24 ~

Guided

Joseph Pearce

Hail Holy Queen, Mother of Mercy,
Our Life, Our Sweetness, and Our Hope;
To thee do we cry, poor banished children of Eve;
To thee do we send up our sighs,
Mourning and weeping in this vale of tears. . . .

On first appearance, it might seem that hope is the least important of the theological virtues. Love, it seems, is far greater. St. Paul tells us that love is the greatest of virtues, and that those who "have not love" are nothing but "a resounding gong or a clanging cymbal," and that those who "have a faith that can move mountains, but have not love" are "nothing." Faith also appears to be greater than hope. Even faith as small as a mustard seed can move mighty mountains. Hope would seem destined to live in the shadow of its more illustrious brethren. It does so in humility, not merely in its willingness to be the servant of the servants of God but in its knowledge that "the last will be first, and the first last."

150

As with the Trinity at the heart of reality, the theological virtues are One even as they are Three. Like their source, of which they are a reflection and a type, they exhibit the divine egalitarianism. If, therefore, hope is the least of the virtues, it is, paradoxically, the least among equals. This convoluted paradox is exemplified by the fact that hope, as the "least" of the virtues, is the antidote to the poison of pride, the greatest of sins. Hope, as the humblest of the virtues, overthrows pride with humility. Where hope prevails, pride fails. Conversely, where hope is absent, pride prevails. Hopelessness is despair, and despair is the triumph of pride. Hope, the humble David of the virtues, slays the mighty Goliath of sins.

Hope also has a special place in pagan mythology, a place reserved for it in Pandora's Box. In point of fact, the box was not Pandora's at all. It belonged to the gods, and she had no right to open it. As with Eve's plucking of the forbidden fruit, Pandora, the pagan Eve, opens the forbidden box. The curse of this original sin plagues humanity as, like a cloud of locusts, vice and disease pour forth from the opened casket. Only hope remains in the box, the silver lining in the cloud that overshadows fallen humanity.

There is so much truth to be discovered in the myth of Pandora's Box that it's a shame that "myth" is so often used as a synonym for "lie." A lie is always a lie, but a myth is often true. I happen to believe in Pandora's Box, not merely because of the metaphors and allegories to be found in it, but because I once found myself actually living in it. Many years ago, or once upon a time, I found myself alone in a prison cell. It was during my own dark ages, before I was received into the Catholic Church. I was a leading member of a white supremacist organization, an angry young man, who had been sentenced to twelve months in prison for "publishing material likely to incite racial hatred." It was during the first days of my sentence. I was in solitary confinement. I was alone; utterly, unspeakably alone. Or so I imagined. I was in fact surrounded by my own vices, my own sins, my own bitterness, my own hates. A plethora of plague-ridden doubts besieged me. My prison cell *was* Pandora's Box.

> *It was hope that formed the mumbled, barely articulate prayers in my mind.*

I had no faith, so I thought. I had no love, except for that love for family and friends that even publicans and sinners have. And yet, hidden somewhere in the corner of my Pandora's Box was the barest flicker of hope. Someone had sent me a rosary. I had no idea what to do with it. I was not a Catholic, though the reading of Chesterton and Belloc had led me closer to the arms of Mother Church than I realized. I didn't know the Hail Mary or the Apostles' Creed or the Glory Be. I had been taught the Our Father many years earlier, at school, but had long since forgotten it. I had never prayed before in my life. What was I to do with this string of beads? It was then, in the midst of "the earthquake, wind, and fire" of my sinful passions, that I heard that whispering hope, the "still, small voice of calm" that would exorcise the demons and still the waters of my heart. It was hope that guided my fingers from bead to bead; it was hope that formed the mumbled, barely articulate prayers in my mind. It was hope that brought me the first inklings of the peace to be found in Christ. It was hope that taught me humility. It was with this thinnest thread of hope in my hands that I climbed downward to my knees.

That was a long time ago. I have long since learned to say the rosary. I have long since learned to honor the Mother of God with the many anthems sung in her honor. I have come to understand that she is the one who allowed God himself to repair the damage done by Eve (and Pandora). She is truly "our life, our sweetness, and our hope." And I have learned that hope is the very sweetness of our life.

> *Turn then, most gracious advocate,*
> *Thine eyes of mercy towards us,*
> *And after this our exile,*
> *Show unto us the blessed fruit of thy womb, Jesus.*

∽ 25 ∾

Seen

Harold Fickett

The invitation to write about hope came in the mail on the day I learned that a book I had been working on for five years would probably never be published. I opened the letter and rushed out of the house to pick up the kids at school, stopping at a gas station on the way. While the gas was pumping into the tank, the dark irony of the book's failure and this writing invitation caught me, and I put my forehead against the steering wheel and began laughing, long and hard. Five years wasted! I might as well sell insurance. Or answer the call to write about *hope*.

My hope registers in such divine winks in the midst of trouble — "hints and guesses" T. S. Eliot calls them. Was the essay invitation such a signal, pointing me away from feeling abandoned by God, even though I received it as a mixed blessing? Right then I wanted to indulge in self-pity, if not outright despair. These emotions and their empty satisfactions depend on a real conviction that one is alone, however. Through this invitation God seemed to be saying, to paraphrase Jesus' statement to Nathanael: I see you under that fig tree.

◆ ◆ ◆

Once I had the good fortune to be sitting on a dais next to Annie Dillard at the kick-off dinner of a literary conference. We had a great time together, chatting about the evangelical jingles we most enjoyed. We both loved "Living for Jesus," and we sang it together *sotto voce* against the din of cutlery and competing conversations. I was about to deliver a speech, and, as usual, I was being carried ever higher by an adrenaline tidal wave that threatened to wash out in a massive flop sweat. When Annie asked me how I was feeling, I told her I was scared. We discussed the specifics of the complaint. She offered that I was not so much frightened as I was lonely.

I've puzzled on what she said for a long time. I've come to the conclusion that the fear and loneliness we feel stems naturally from our status as vulnerable creatures and supernaturally as a consequence of our alienation from God. When God walked out with our first parents in the evening, the Scriptures tell us, humankind knew no such poverty of spirit. With sin came the terrible absence, the terrible need, the unspeakable longing. It asserts itself, at least in my case, when I feel I'm about to reveal my inadequacies before too many eyes. What a poor naked animal I am.

Yet I am assured, from small signs in my own life to the far more substantial and reliable testimony of the Scriptures, that I am not alone. Jesus promised to be with his followers to the end and send a Comforter as the minister of the psalmist's "very present help in trouble." My brokenness still wars, though, against the new creature I am in Christ.

When I pray I like to go into the chapel of my local parish and kneel down before the reserved sacrament, where the sanctuary lamp — its flame constant — signals the Lord's presence in the high altar's tabernacle. "The Lord is in his holy temple," I say, "let us keep silence before him." And then, "My Lord and my God." In a life that continues to be one long high-wire act I find a genuine peace. The Lord *is* in his holy temple. I am not alone. I can dare to imagine that I am loved.

"This fear in a handful of dust," as Eliot names humanity, is somehow precious to God. Although I cannot begin to fathom God, I can't miss the crucifix to the left of the altar. The death Jesus died, and the alienation from the Son that the Father endured, declares God's loving character.

To the right of the altar stands a statue of Jesus with his arms raised as if about to extend a sheltering embrace. Often, before I leave the chapel, I'll stand beside it and think of a line from St. Andrew's feast day: "The Lord loved Andrew and cherished his friendship." I pray the same is true of me.

So I live my life not alone but as one member of Jesus' company. My own keeping company with Jesus is amplified and given concrete expression in innumerable ways through my fellow believers. They ask me how I'm doing. They tell me I'm not so much afraid as feeling alone. They assure me that I need be neither — that I am certainly not alone. Jesus and his company give me the ability to hope, and hope is the great antidote to fear and loneliness.

Hope allows us to believe that there are solutions to our problems that we ourselves cannot yet imagine. Hope gives us the patience to wait while "all things work together for good to them that love God" (Rom. 8:28, KJV). God makes all things work together for good for those who love him.

◆ ◆ ◆

The great twentieth-century musician Olivier Messiaen composed one of the last century's greatest pieces of music. Captured by the Nazis at the beginning of World War II and sent to a prisoner-of-war camp in Silesia, Messiaen responded by composing *The Quartet for the End of Time*. Its movements express humankind's beginning in paradise, the sin of our first parents, Christ's advent, the groaning of creation for its redemption, and the consummation of all things in a new heaven and a new earth, where God will be all in all. Messiaen suffered the rest of his life from the malnourishment he experienced during his imprisonment. He lived in a cold barracks and could barely see beyond the camp's walls, and yet he grasped by faith an ultimate reconciliation.

Hope is the antidote to loneliness — to self-pity and despair. As Dante concludes the *Paradiso,* "My will and my desire were turned by love, / The love that moves the sun and the other stars." In my dark moments, even when I'd rather God leave me alone, He turns "my will and my desire" back toward him with a thoughtful gesture — such as an invitation to write about hope — and reminds me that whatever I may be thinking and feeling, God remains greater than the universe itself, much less my small troubles. Yet he cares about them too.

∼ 26 ∼

Rejuvenate!
Timothy Radcliffe, O.P.

For many Catholics, this is indeed a difficult time. We do not seem to be advancing toward the church we had dreamed of after the Second Vatican Council; there is polarization, especially in the United States; there is distrust between clergy and laity and, in many dioceses, between the clergy and their bishops. There have been the terrible scandals of sexual abuse. This is indeed a time of crisis. How can we hope?

First of all we must recognize that Christianity is founded upon crises and finds in them sources of life and rejuvenation. The greatest crisis that our church ever faced was on the night before Jesus died. In *What Is the Point of Being a Christian?* (Burns & Oates, 2005), I have argued that this was the night upon which the disciples lost the plot. They had gone up to Jerusalem hoping that Jesus would be recognized as Messiah, but at the Last Supper it became clear that this was not going to happen, and so they all began to plan their exit strategies.

159

Time and again, our sacrament of hope brings us back to this founding story of our community, when there was no story of the future to tell (when there was no hope).

And then came the second great crisis that the church endured: the failure of Jesus to come again in glory. It was this second loss of a story of the future that drove the early Christians to wrestle with the meaning of what they had lived and to write the Gospels. Jesus did indeed come, not with angels and trumpet blasts, but in Matthew, Mark, Luke, and John.

So we need not be afraid of crisis. The foundational story of our church, the Last Supper, teaches that we may go into the dark night and lose God, but this is only so that we may find God closer to us than we had ever imagined. And is our present crisis really so great? Think back a hundred years. Pius X had recently become pope. He was vigorously centralizing the church and suppressing "dissent." In 1907 he began his onslaught against the new theology, with its historical understanding of Scripture, publishing the terrible encyclicals *Lamentabili* and *Pascendi,* attacking "Modernism." And go back another hundred years, to 1807: Napoleon was about to capture Rome, dioceses were without bishops, the Jesuits were suppressed. Today there is hardly a church in Europe that does not claim that it was then turned into a stable by the emperor. Religious life was almost extinct.

Comparatively, we are living through a minor crisis. Perhaps it seems so awful because the Second Vatican

Council raised the hopes of many Catholics so high. We believed that in a short while the church would be deeply renewed, less centralized, less clerical; and that has not happened. At the same time we are living through a wider crisis caused by the loss of confidence in progress. For two hundred years our society was powered by the conviction that it was evolving inevitably for the good. This is no longer evident. Progress, the secular faith of recent centuries, can no longer be assumed.

There is the rise of religious terrorism, the spread of AIDS. Many states in Africa are threatened with collapse. We are storing nuclear weapons that could destroy the world. We are living through a climate change that threatens our lives and that is directly the responsibility of the West. In the face of all this, what word of hope do we have for humanity?

If it turns out that our Christian hope is just the sprinkling of holy water on secular trust in progress, then the future is indeed bleak. But if we can rediscover the core Christian hope that passes through death and resurrection, the hope of the Last Supper, then we shall have something wonderful to offer each other and all people in this uncertain time.

◆ ◆ ◆

On the night before he died, Jesus did not tell the disciples how things would work out after his death and resurrection. He left them with no road map of the future.

Instead he performed a sign. He took bread, broke it, and blessed it and shared it with the disciples, saying "This is my body, given for you." When no future was imaginable, it spoke of hope. When the community was coming to bits, it spoke of a new covenant. When they were all busy disengaging from the Lord, getting ready to deny him or run away, it spoke of forgiveness.

> *Christianity is founded upon crises and finds in them sources of life and rejuvenation.*

We need signs that speak of our hope. I have just returned from Zimbabwe, a country crucified by poverty and oppression. In some places, 40 percent of the population is HIV positive. I visited a small clinic called Mashambanzou, a simple place of tin and brick sheds run by religious sisters. The name means "the dawn," but its literal meaning is "when the elephants wash." Dawn is when the elephants go to the river and play and squirt water at each other. It is the time of joy. And this clinic was a place of the dawn. We played with the children, all of whom are AIDS orphans. One of our Dominican sisters had lost three of her six siblings to AIDS. She told me that they all died at dawn.

Vaclav Havel wrote that "hope is not the conviction that something will turn out well, but the certainty that something makes sense, regardless of how it turns out." Our hope is not an optimism that all will be fine, that somehow we shall find a solution to our global crises. Our hope is that our histories, individual and communal, will ultimately be found to have meaning; that our victories and defeats, our sins and moments of virtue, will stand as part of a story in which meaninglessness will not have the last word. We can get only small glimpses of the plot, that ultimate narrative, but God is writing it, and it is the book of life.

～ 27 ～

Incredible

Robert Royal

"That they see how things go today and believe that things will be better tomorrow morning. . . . I am astonished by it myself. My grace must really be of incredible force." This is the — not exactly ironic — opinion of none other than God himself in Charles Péguy's poem on hope, *Le porche du mystère du deuxième vertu,* written early in the twentieth century, even before the cataclysms that we think, in retrospect, have made hope so much more difficult in our time. How can you write poetry after Auschwitz, we've been told, or how can we labor for a better future when we have seen the collapse of all the modern progressive faiths? I do not entirely know how to answer these questions, but I am quite certain they do not have much to do with the real virtue of hope.

Péguy's God thought Faith was easy. He had put so much of Himself into Creation that it was hard not to believe, He imagined, unless you deliberately blinded yourself. And Charity, at least in principle, was easier still.

164

How can we not feel compassion for one another, given the tragic Pascalian distance between our intuition of the grandeur that a human life might be and our knowledge of the misery in which all of us, regularly, find ourselves? Hope, though, is a tough nut, and always has been. In all of literature, there is probably no other instance of God pronouncing his own action incredible. Yet Péguy knew what he was about in pursuing the specific nature of hope. Wars and rumors of wars, the death of children, the inconstancy of love, the indifference of nature, the list goes on and on. And he did not live to see much of the twentieth century.

We should not exaggerate the uniqueness of our own day, however. To begin with, it is a very good thing to lose false hopes, which is what the old modern optimism about humankind and progress really were. In the ancient Greek myth, Pandora opens a forbidden box and, like her non-pagan counterpart Eve, releases all evils into the world. Only one thing remained under the lid: *elpis,* or hope. Unlike the hope of Adam and Eve in Genesis, though, Pandora's hope shares some characteristics with the other ills in the box, not least that it holds out false promises that make it possible for the human race to be tormented over and over again by false expectations: hopes in the plural that belong to a different, delusive category than does the Christian hope that is always in the singular.

That grammatical difference makes all the spiritual difference in the world. Because true hope, which is to say Christian hope, is singular, a comprehensive orientation. As such it does not depend on successes in the normal sense of the word. To speak from my own experience, it is all but impossible to say how this particular virtue gets communicated to us. It's a virtue because it seems habitual in the old scholastic sense of being a steady disposition, even though we do not have it at our command. That is why it may be even more difficult to say why our virtue of hope does not crumble under repeated trials. But even if we cannot explain how hope takes up residence in us and is sustained there, we do know that it is not a kind of "life force" in the way that biologistic theories over the past two centuries have tried to make it appear. Hope operates under a different sky — day and night — than do survival strategies and successful projects.

To the purely secular mind, this kind of talk is, of course, the purest nonsense. It seems built on the thinnest air. It pulls no weight in economics or politics. It sounds like the kind of thing that Oprah and other purveyors of uplift spout daily to people desperate for some reason to believe their lives matter. It gets us involved in the kinds of empty play of words with which, some believe, theologians and philosophers have mystified themselves for millennia. You have to be almost brain dead not to see the massive evidence that denies hope.

Even to the eye of a believer, all this and more seems only too probable at times.

Indeed, the church herself quite often does not seem to offer much reason for hope — except when you compare it with everything else. No nation on earth has had as intelligent and forceful leaders in the past thirty years as John Paul II and Benedict XVI. Compared with the Mother Teresas of the world, the secular saviors seem like small potatoes. Yes, we do not build beautiful churches or compose moving music or even conduct dignified liturgies for the most part; and priests and bishops have let us down, not least in the abuse of children. Still, where does the world turn for moral guidance and examples of good living? Not to the White House or the Elysée Palace, and certainly not to the United Nations or European Union. The collapse of ideologies has made us much more modest in our expectations of public authorities. To some people, this is an unfortunate development. For those who understand hope, though, it marks the return of "put not your trust in princes."

It would be pretty to think that public authorities could somehow participate in the glories of the kingdom. But we pine for this fantasy because we no longer read Augustine or the mainstream of our tradition with sympathy. The old North African was just too pessimistic about human nature, we think. He and those like him are responsible for those old church views about this being a vale of tears and our lives a spiritual combat, about ne-glecting this world for promises of the next. In America today we know that life is a moveable feast, that people are "basically good," that a "normal" human life is one in which everyone has an interesting and well-paying job and troubles only come when greedy persons in corpo-rations or corrupt politicians disturb the natural order of happiness and contentment.

There is also much talk about the values of the Enlightenment. But along with many real gains, the En-lightenment brought a substantial loss of realism about the human condition, an impoverishment that has led to much unhappiness. We thought we could do without things like the virtue of hope because we would build a world in which hopes could be satisfied. But the old intuitions about human nature and human society have proven more durable and closer to the truth than the new hopes. We have God's promise, however incredible it sometimes seems; and that ultimate hope imperfectly, by fits and starts, wounded and misconstrued though it be, puts our other hopes and dreams into an entirely different perspective.

I have always been struck by the verses in Psalm 64: "You keep your pledge with wonder, O God our Savior, the hope of all the earth and of far distant isles." What was the psalmist thinking? If God is the hope of all the earth, what are the distant isles doing there? Is this just a bit of Hebrew pleonasm? Perhaps it is just a bit of space-age fantasy on my part, but it strikes me that even on the moon, or among the stars — the most distant isles of all — hope in God's constant pledge will be what really keeps us going. And if, with Péguy's God, that force astonishes us, well, that is just one more reason why we need and will find hope.

With Emily

Robert Imbelli

Perhaps no poet writing in English is so cryptic and tan-
talizing as Emily Dickinson. And few of her poems equal
the following in that regard:

> It might be lonelier
> Without the Loneliness —
> I'm so accustomed to my Fate —
> Perhaps the Other — Peace —
>
> Would interrupt the Dark —
> And crowd the little Room —
> Too scant — by Cubits — to contain
> The Sacrament — of Him —
>
> I am not used to Hope —
> It might intrude upon —
> Its sweet parade — blaspheme the place —
> Ordained to Suffering —

It might be easier
To fail — with Land in Sight —
Than gain — My Blue Peninsula —
To perish — of Delight —

Dickinson evokes the paradoxical, though perhaps not uncommon, sensation that hope can be deeply unsettling, even unselfing. Thus it is often safer to trim our sails: to settle for the already colonized island of *expectation* than to risk the ever receding shore of *hope.*

For, with expectation, we remain securely in control. We can keep the door bolted shut, or opened but a crack; able to decide who or what to let in or keep out. After all, our room is small, the self comfortably constricted. And the dark, like the tomb, offers its own uncomplicated consolation.

So we see Mary Magdalene, spurred on by duty and desire, making her way to the tomb, "while it was still dark" (John 20:1). She expected to perform the solemn rites for the dead, bearing ointments and spices to anoint the body of Jesus (Mark 16:1).

We make haste to celebrate her and the other women as heroic heralds of glad tidings. But before proclaiming her "apostle to the apostles" (in Augustine's generous phrase), it would be well to dwell upon Mary's prior distress: no dead body to anoint. A Holy Saturday, spent in single-minded expectation, yields to fear and resentment: Where have they taken the Lord?

"Why do you expect to find the living One among the dead?" (Luke 24:5) comes the disconcerting query. It does, indeed, intrude upon the place, "ordained to suffering," and jealously preserved lest worse befall. The loneliness of mourning made even lonelier by an empty tomb.

Mary of Magdala's new birth from expectation to hope required, in John's telling, a double "turning," a double conversion. Turning, she saw him and thought him the gardener. Then, beyond all expectation, she heard her name: "Maria." Turning a second time, she knew him: "Rabbouni!" (see John 20:14–16). A new creation comes in sight, but its cost is a twice-exposed vulnerability.

The church's liturgy honors Mary Magdalene in the ancient Easter sequence, *Victimae Paschali Laudes.* The ode addresses her directly: "Tell us, Mary, what did you see?" And she replies: *"Surrexit Christus, spes mea / praecedet vos in Galilaeam;"* "Christ, my hope, is risen / he goes before you into Galilee."

Hope, for the Christian, bears the form and face of the risen Christ. Not an abstract virtue, it only arises from personal encounter with Jesus the Christ. The First Letter of Peter urges beleaguered believers of the first century: "Always be prepared to give an account of the hope that is in you to all who ask, doing so with gentleness and reverence" (1 Pet. 3:15). And Peter makes clear that the basis of their hope is the resurrection of Jesus from the dead. Though they have not physically seen him, yet they love and believe in him "with unutterable and exalted joy" (1 Pet. 1:8). Thus faith and hope stand inextricably intertwined. Absent faith, hope ever risks regressing to mere expectation.

Through the centuries the personal encounter that continues to nourish Christian hope transpires, of course, in the Eucharist: at once remembrance, presence, and promise. To the eyes of faith the Eucharist is the true "Sacrament of Him," intimated in Dickinson's poem.

A contemporary poet, Mary Karr, espies more than distant traces — the Blue Peninsular of Dickinson's dreams. Karr's own poem, "Disgraceland" (in the collection *Sinners Welcome*), revels in a robust, non-sentimental sacramentality. Recounting her personal journey, she confesses:

> Eventually, I lurched out
>   to kiss the wrong mouths, get stewed,
>
> and sulk around. Christ always stood
>   to one side with a glass of water.
>   I swatted the sap away.
>
> When my thirst got great enough to ask,
>   a stream welled up inside,
>   some jade wave buoyed me forward,
>
> and I found myself upright
>   in the instant, with a garden
>   inside my own ribs aflourish.

There, the arbor leafs.
 The vines push out plump grapes.
  You are loved, someone said. Take that

 and eat it.

"Christ, my hope, is risen," exclaims Magdalene; "he goes before you." Christ always precedes the believer on the way; yet he is mysteriously met in his sisters and brothers, especially those most in need. "I was hungry and you gave me food, thirsty and you gave me drink" (Matt. 25:35). Just as the Eucharist is always *viaticum,* food for the ongoing journey of faith, so the hope the risen Christ engenders is never comfortable possession, always both gift and task.

Those gifted with the ultimate hope of sharing Christ's resurrected life bear particular responsibility for bringing life-giving hope to the afflicted here and now. Thus, to faith and hope, love is joined as trinitarian completion and crown. For Christian service of the other lives from and embodies Paul's faith-filled hope: "I am sure that neither death, nor life, nor angels, nor principalities, nor things present, nor things to come, nor anything else in all creation, will be able to separate us from the love of God in Christ Jesus our Lord" (Rom. 8:38–39).

✥ 29 ✥

Charmed

Jeanine Hathaway

When I was growing up, an enviable accessory to our school uniform was a charm bracelet from the Catholic doodad store. From the silver chain dangled traditional icons for baptism's infused virtues; the heart stood for charity, the cross for faith, the anchor for hope. The cross and the heart were familiar symbols, but the anchor on the charm bracelet, a cross that split into twinned fishhooks, was beyond me. When my family could leave Chicago for vacations, we'd rent a cottage on a little lake nearby, usually in Michigan or Indiana. What I knew of anchors then was limited to a three-pound coffee can of cement on a chain under the seat of a creaky rowboat.

In school, faith and charity were the important virtues to study, to work on. The optimist's license for passivity, hope required neither study nor work, indistinguishable as it was from wishing. I hoped my mother in labor would bring us a brother finally; when she didn't, I understood the fishhooks at the base of that cross. I

175

hoped for a pony for Christmas; fishhooks. I hoped for divine intervention in the form of an A on the algebra final; more fishhooks, though when I squeaked by, just passing the course, I acknowledged not the "fishhook" but the correct nautical term, "fluke." Eventually, on hope's sliding scale, I entered and left religious life. Within four years of each other, two of my eight younger siblings died, suddenly, when we were in our twenties. I entered and left a marriage. The women's movement picked up momentum and my identity, forged pre–Vatican II, was under attack. Attached as I was to that identity, confused by its habitual rightness and obvious wrongness, I began losing hope. The church offered its clichés, dismissible because now understandable, in the vernacular.

My understanding of hope had been about reliance on someone outside myself, the *mysterium tremendum et fascinans* whom experience had revealed to be the capricious *deus absconditus* with a manly will more powerful than mine, an intelligence more logical and legalistic. An ex-nun, ex-wife, single mother, I was supposed to be a virtuous woman, submissive, without hormones, reliable as the Virgin I'd been taught to model, *Ms. Fiat.* Well, no thanks to what I knew of that.

Aquinas says the mind moves toward truth, the will toward good. They cannot do otherwise. In this order of things, the mind assents to faith, the will to charity. There we have the cross and the heart. But I was adrift and floundering and didn't want that anchor which hung like a ball and chain on one easily charged with guilt. What I really wanted was a way out of feeling stuck. For centuries, the church has chanted the "Veni Creator Spiritus" and often meant it. For centuries that Creator Spirit has worked around the patriarchal top-heaviness of the institution. The Creator Spirit looks under the Rock and gives light and air to what lives there by means of symbols, the offerings of the imagination.

Symbols are what reveal to us life in its abundance. It is in their liminality that I find cause to hope. Through them the church teaches us that what something appears to be is only a portal, an introduction to, only the beginning of what it is. To surrender to this is the way into mystery. And mystery is where Wisdom dances on the beach, the playground of the imagination. This, I suspect, is why Simone Weil suggested we teach schoolchildren to meditate, to untether themselves in silence, that graced state, in order to act from a considered awareness of consequence: how we got here, where we're going.

Etymologically, "hope" is thought to come from a word in a Low German dialect, *hop,* meaning "to jump to safety." It doesn't imply that after you jump, you homestead. *Hop* is a verb, kinetic. Inside it is another hop. Imagine trying to hop with an anchor. As change is life's only constant, I propose quitting the anchor image entirely. I don't want to be stuck with the weight.

As we move into the twenty-first century, I meet more people disillusioned by spin, speed, greed; more

people on Prozac, even more self-medicating. Children —
children! — commit suicide because they can't imagine
anything better. So I go back to earlier times, slower and
more local, by nature integrated. And there, in places as
distant from each other as Tibet and Wales, I find another
symbol: the coracle.

The coracle on which I'd pattern my bracelet charm is
the Irish one designed for Boyne River fishing and trans-
port. Basically it's a round wicker basket, four feet in
diameter and eighteen inches deep, covered in a single
watertight cow- or horse-hide. The seat is slung across
the middle, a shoulder brace for portage. The coracle is
propelled by a single-bladed paddle held in both hands
over the bow. The rower uses a figure-eight stroke which,
given the speed of the thing, looks appropriately like our
symbol for infinity. You dig in, you move slowly, learning
where currents (and rapids) are.

The early Irish hermits chose to forego the paddle
entirely, drifting and shooting with God toward the
sea, their version of the desert. They were intention-
ally unbound, without anchor, in infinite water, infinite
possibility. They could read the weather; they spoke the
languages of predator and prey; they hung their cloaks
on sunbeams; one built a cook-fire on the back of a
whale that politely waited till the monk had eaten before
sounding.

What critics call "magical realism" comes out of the literature of traditionally folk-religious Catholic countries,

because anything can happen in a sacramental world. The "magic" is easily understood to be the action of grace. When my schoolmates read the biographies of Amelia Earhart and Henry Ford, I was cozying up to the lives of the saints. Saints could raise the dead, bleed on Fridays, fly to a church beam at the smell of sin, live for years on biscuits brought by trained ravens.

Such stories continue to appeal to the imagination. It is the imagination that prompts the intellect to ask, *Is it true?* and then in the gap between Q and A, the Spirit suggests the zinger: *Could it be?* Call arouses response, a single drumbeat sets us up for a second. As with any seduction, a space opens in which we float a while, carry on a conversation, sort out the goods before moving into action.

The goods include contraries. I have read that the opposite of love is efficiency; the opposite of faith is certainty. We've been taught that the opposite of hope is despair, but in my experience, the opposite of hope is McLife: fast, filling, without surprise, and not good for us or our home planet. Contraries are at the extremes of a living continuum, necessary to balance a living paradox.

In lowercase catholic, we learn from other cultures. Koshares, the Hopi clowns, embody contradiction, paradoxical extremes. In ceremonies of tremendous significance, these are gluttonous men nearly naked but for their two-horned headgear, pouch of prayer meal, loincloth, and mismatched footwear, in recent years sometimes high-top sneakers. Their skin is painted in black and white stripes. The colors do not converge; there is no gray area from head to high-top. Koshares are annoying. They make fun of ritual, interrupting solemnity with ribaldry, charging the very air with tension. When spectators take photos, koshares leap into the crowd, snatch the cameras and take pictures of the hapless photographers. They gobble huge slices of watermelon, letting the juice drip all over themselves and everyone else. Crazy-making, they dramatize the self-restoring imagination, homeostatic truth taking action. They have the hard work of reminding their people to let go.

What's the point of hoping that life will be controllable? As Thich Nhat Hanh writes, "We are not in control but we are in charge." And so in charge, I'll keep the nautical theme but change the symbol. I don't want to be weighed down by nostalgia — or any other form that fear takes. Stay buoyant, says hope; clown around. This is the moment to shape infinity with the paddle that's in your hands.

∼ 30 ∼

Full Spectrum
Philip Zaleski

As a child, I knew that virtues had colors. Faith was blue, a match for sky and ocean, the two infinities that surround us, fill us, and define our horizon; charity was red, the bright scarlet of martyr's blood, the pale rose of friendship; and hope — well, hope was green, something that, when properly nourished, blossomed into flowers blue and red, into a fuller faith and, God willing, even into love.

This spectrum progressed, in my imagining, from blue to green to red. Faith came first. I had many friends, it was true, who had no religion to speak of and even scoffed at the cross and the six-pointed star, the two holy symbols in my young world, but at the same time I saw that my companions knew the meaning of trust, had known it from birth, as a thorough confidence in their own family, in their mother and father, and that this knowing was a palpable intimation of faith. Hope, too, seemed inborn, an instinct, at least in my friends and me, who hoped (because we trusted) every year that Santa Claus would fill our stockings, that our favorite team would win the pennant, that God would grant us eternal life (this being, of course, a portion of the proper theological understanding of hope). As for charity, that was a more difficult matter. In my family love abounded, but in the world it was hit or miss. Everyone loved love, but not everyone knew love.

As an adult, three or four decades removed from these speculations, my youthful palette of virtues seems to possess not only its share of beauty but a good degree of truth. Granted, it needs clarification; I now know, for example, that the church understands faith, hope, and love as infused virtues, implanted directly within each of us by God. What I like most about my spectrum, though, is that its imaginative progression from blue through green to red flows against the natural spectrum, at least as customarily presented in scientific texts, which portray the electromagnetic radiation of visible light as a gradation of decreasing wavelengths from red (700 nanometers) through green (550 nanometers) to blue (450 nanometers). My reversal of the natural sequence seems entirely fitting, bearing in mind Jesus' saying that "in the world ye shall have tribulation; but be of good cheer; I have overcome the world" (John 16:33). It suggests that we, who are of the world, are meant to see all things in a light that comes from beyond the world, to remember always the promises of Our Lord and the power of love to overcome all, even death; to recall, as Aragorn says in the film version of that great Catholic classic *Lord of the Rings,* "There is always hope" — a bold restatement of the novel's more poetically suggestive "Dawn is ever the hope of men" (*The Two Towers,* Book III, Chapter VII).

There is always hope. I have seen this many times: In my dying father, who managed to overcome alcoholism while cancer crept through his body, and who, for the first time in years, faced his future — which was his death — with clear eyes; in an elderly woman I knew who persevered for decades to bring illumination to the minds of recalcitrant young men and women, and who once told me that "despair is always a failure to see things clearly"; in a good friend who climbed the ladder from heroin addiction to hope in Christ. *There is always hope.* I have seen this truth in great literature; in Herbert's "I gave to hope a watch of mine but he / An anchor gave to me"; in Dame Julian's "All will be well," echoed so beautifully by Eliot in his *Four Quartets;* in Crashaw's "Dear Hope! earth's dowry, and heaven's debt." I have seen it most memorably in Dante's *Commedia,* and there where it is least expected. The gates to Inferno famously declare "Abandon all hope, you who enter here," and yet the denizens of Hell manifest hope, or its infernal counterpart, for they fret constantly about their reputations on earth, the fate of their families, the future of their beloved or despised Florence. This is not eschatological hope, but it is participation in the movement of life and a real, if twisted, desire for the good. In Purgatory, of course, hope is everywhere, it is the great song of all the inhabitants, exemplified in the *Te lucis ante terminum,* the celebrated compline hymn, radiant with hope, sung near the entrance to Purgatory proper:

> Before the ending of the day
> Creator of the world, we pray
> That you with your clemency
> May be our guardian and keeper.

Only in Paradise, where the Beatific Vision eternally unfolds, does hope vanish, to be replaced by joyful certainty. It is in heaven that a sign should read: Abandon all hope, you who enter here. For if hope is, as the Letter to the Hebrews suggests, a matter of "things unseen" yet anticipated in faith, then in heaven hope has no place, for all is seen, all is known, all has reached fruition.

But we are not yet in heaven. Here on earth hope is as vital to our existence as food, drink, or air. It is, moreover, an obligation, a demand that Christ places upon all his followers, as the response of the will to the exigencies of life. What does this tell us about our situation today? The life of the Catholic Church in the twenty-first century is what it has always been: dark and bright, peopled by sinners and by saints, on the verge of ruin yet unshakeable in its foundations, a bureaucratic morass yet a holy temple, in sum a sacred mystery, and we who encounter Christ in the Catholic Church have no choice but to be radiant with hope. As Paul writes in an extraordinary passage that refers to many things, above all to the hope of the resurrection, but that can be read also as an account of our present need as Catholics in a time of crisis, "We know that the whole creation groaneth and travaileth in pain together until now. And not only they, but ourselves also, which have the firstfruits of the Spirit, even we ourselves groan within ourselves, waiting for the adoption, to wit, the redemption of our body" (Rom. 8:22–23, KJV). What is the way out of this travail? Where do we turn? To Christ, yes, but in what way? Paul answers for all time those who know anxiety and sorrow and fear in his very next sentence: "For we are saved by hope."

And to that, what can we reply, as we orient our being along the supernatural spectrum of virtues, except: Lord, grant us the love that is the consummation of faith, the resolution of hope, the alpha and omega of the Christian life?

～ 31 ～

Out and Back
Paul Mariani

I am at the moment foundering in a mass of details as I try to construct a viable portrait of Gerard Manley Hopkins, that nineteenth-century English Jesuit who in his relatively short life (he died before reaching his forty-fifth birthday), had it about as hard as most of us will ever have it. Writing of the wreck of the German steamship *The Deutschland* off the mouth of the Thames in December 1875, Fr. Hopkins meditated on the hard deaths of a quarter of the ship's passengers and crew, among them five Franciscan nuns exiled under the Bismarck regime who had been posted to a place they would never reach: St. Louis, Missouri. Rockets, flares, a beacon onshore signaling back. Help expected hour after hour as the storm lifted and smashed the ship against a treacherous sand bar as if playing with it, and no aid forthcoming. *Hope*, Hopkins sighed,

> *had grown grey hairs,*
> *Hope had mourning on,*

186

Trenched with tears, carved with cares,
Hope was twelve hours gone;
And frightful a nightfall folded rueful a day
Nor rescue, only rocket and lightship, shone,
And lives at last were washing away:
To the shrouds they took, — they shook in the hurling and
      horrible airs.

No Saturday matinee rescue, nothing. Nothing but salt brine and "wiry and white-fiery and whirlwind-swivellèd snow" and numbing cold. Abandonment, the captain and the crew helpless in the face of the storm though some passengers tried to climb into the rigging and hold on and could not and fell into the pulverizing waves. The cries of children, of mothers, of passengers being washed overboard, some throwing themselves into the sea rather than wait for the inevitable. Nothing for it, then, but despair.

But, no. Something. One of the nuns calling out into the freezing dark for her Lord, for Christ to come, and come quickly. *Maranatha.* The ancient cry. Christ on the cross, a Jew crying out the words of the ancient Psalm, "My God, my God, why have you forsaken me?!" An interrobang, I imagine, if interrobangs had existed in David's time: a question and a cry of bewilderment at one and the same time.

For weeks now, as I've moved through Lent, I have been reciting to myself lines that Hopkins composed in the last year of his life, as he meditated on what he summed up as the massive disappointments of his life. His failure to produce the academic papers he had hoped to write. His belief that he would ultimately fail in the work he did in teaching and tutoring young English and Irish Catholics in a time when they were at a distinct disadvantage in getting into the best British universities because of their faith; his failure to get his extraordinary poems a hearing even among his fellow Jesuits or his closest friends, among them three published poets, including a future poet laureate. The relentless passage of time with nothing — ultimately — to show for it. The growing sense of all humanity's being swallowed up in the new geological and chronological immensities of Darwin and Lyell and Huxley, where all of civilization was fast on its way to being in an "enormous dark / Drowned" And now he himself — like the nuns he had sung of a dozen years earlier — shipwrecked, without hope.

And yet, in the midst of all that: the memory of God's promise that he would not abandon us, as he had not finally abandoned his Son on the cross. The hope that death itself — which we all fear — had been defeated and that the sacrifice of the cross had lifted not only Christ, but all those who would only hold onto his garment, by which they might steal heaven and be lifted up with the One who had taken on our humanity so that we might take on his divinity. "Enough!" Hopkins wrote in the last year of his life, echoing Paul's promise to the community at Corinth:

> *the Resurrection,*
> *A heart's-clarion! Away grief's gasping, | joyless days, dejection.*
> *Across my foundering deck shone*
> *A beacon, an eternal beam. | Flesh fade, and mortal trash*
> *Fall to the residuary worm; | world's wildfire, leave but ash:*
> *In a flash, at a trumpet crash,*
> *I am all at once what Christ is, | since he was what I am, and*
> *This Jack, joke, poor potsherd, | patch, matchwood, immortal diamond,*
> *Is immortal diamond.*

It's been a hard time, these past few years, what with the church abuse scandals and the daily news coming out of Afghanistan and Iraq, as earlier it came out of Bosnia and Rwanda and Cambodia and Beirut and Vietnam and Korea and Treblinka, and Auschwitz. But then I think of the faces of John Paul and of Benedict, of their words and actions, of their continual call to hope, and I am consoled. I think of my own parish, its members growing older, and of the hope I feel in the crying and fidgeting of those babies the young couples bring to Mass. I think of the Seder I shared with my neighbors, of good food and laughter, of all we hold in common. I think of the example of my wife and sons, and of the deep joy my grandchildren give me just by being.

I think too of the essential goodness of people, of the peace most of us desire. I think of God going before and

after his people — the good, the indifferent, the inca-
pacitated, the petty thieves and psychopaths — as they
wandered the desert year after year, being prepared to
come at last into a land of milk and honey, even if the
journey out took forty years. For humility and patience
and wisdom must go before and follow after hope. A
rising and a falling and a rising: the age-old pattern repeated over and over. The turn in the spiral stairwell,
and the host waiting at the end, as he waited at the
beginning.

∾ 32 ∽

L'Esperança
Valerie Sayers

Wandering through the starkly beautiful fourteenth-century Eglésia de Santa María del Mar in Barcelona recently, I found myself drawn to a simple and vibrant bare wooden statue of Mary. I stood admiring it for a minute or two before I thought to lean in and read the wall plaque which named her, in Catalan, *Mare de Déu de l'Esperança:* Our Lady of Hope. This Mary, energetic and strong in precisely the way young mothers need to be, stars dancing round her head, looked as if she might burst into dance herself. She radiated hope.

I found it a strange coincidence that of all the statuary in a large Gothic church, I was drawn to Our Lady of Hope, when only weeks before my mother had described a vivid dream about her. My mother suffers from macular degeneration. For years she managed to maintain good vision in one eye, until one morning when she looked in the mirror and discovered a large black hole where her face should have been. She had suffered a hemorrhage in her good eye overnight. The experience must have been devastating — suddenly she could neither drive nor read — but every time I talked to her, she exuded optimism and good cheer.

It was only after her dream that she allowed how bleak and despairing she had sometimes felt in those early days after the hemorrhage. In her dream, she told me, Mary appeared holding something hidden in her closed hand and announced that she had a gift. "What is it? What is it?" my mother asked. "It is the most valuable thing I can give you," Mary told her. "It is hope."

My mother is famous among her children for dreams that resemble parables or prophecies or both. Once, in twilight sleep as she was about to give birth, she dreamed that God begged her to please take over for him, an overwhelming vision of motherhood that I borrowed to use in a novel's childbirth scene. When she recounted her dream about Mary, she offered me a vision of hope that was both surprising and oddly familiar. A few years back, between a diagnosis of melanoma and a clean bill of health, I too had nighttime visitations and hopeful dreams. Back then, I found myself invoking hope a thousand times a day: "Hope costs nothing," I chanted to myself. "Where there is despair." . . .

So hope was something of an old friend when I stood in front of the statue. And yet, much as I admired my mother's boundless hopefulness, I had lately forgotten how to be hopeful myself. Maybe it seemed more natural (or perhaps I was better trained) to ask for willed, personal hope — hope to battle unexpected disease, to accept grace when it arrives — than to pray for the kind of hope I needed when I was convinced that church and country were driving me to distracted hopelessness. Lately I had even felt myself living in the Age of Despair, a time of group hopelessness, my friends and colleagues as overwhelmed as I by a government and church we experienced as increasingly authoritarian, focused on sexual repression, disconnected from those suffering the most. "Hanging on by my toenails," I would tell friends who inquired whether I was still a practicing Catholic.

Maybe it was quite natural that hope for the institutional church would not come easily to me. I have been a rebellious Catholic since childhood, as full of myself as I have been full of criticism for the church. As a girl, I used to self-righteously complain that our parish priests ought to be helping the poor instead of throwing cocktail parties and redecorating the rectory. My father once suggested that I run for pope, so I could properly straighten everybody out, and even as a ten-year-old I could recognize the multiple ironies of *that* idea.

But critical though I have always been, I was still a Catholic, wandering a basilica in Barcelona, and there was Our Lady of Hope, stopping me in my tracks. I hadn't fully realized until that moment that maybe I was in Barcelona looking for hope. I thought — and here more ironies pile up — that I was in Barcelona looking for anarchists, or at least for a better sense of their history. It was the Spanish anarchists, strangely enough, who helped me find a way to be in the church when I was my most rebellious post-adolescent self. In graduate school I had become intrigued by the anarchist collectives of early twentieth-century Spain, with their sense of justice, their generosity and egalitarianism, their devotion to the most direct democracy possible.

But at the time I discovered them, I was in pretty desperate need of God and I was also probing pacifist notions, and the Spanish anarchists were not about to illuminate either. They did, however, lead me to explore another group that has sometimes defined itself as anarchist: the Catholic Worker movement, a collective that managed to reconcile egalitarianism, justice for the poor, and commitment to peace with religious faith. Their presence in the church convinced me that there might even be a place for a carping seeker like myself.

So in my youth the Spanish anarchists had led me along a circuitous route to a home in the church, and now in middle age I stood in a church that had been gutted — twice — by Spanish anarchists lashing out against the closest, most visible seat of power and privilege: the church.

I am my mother's daughter, a dreamer of dreams and diviner of portents. I know there are a dozen ironic ways I could read that statue in Barcelona — but I chose to read it in precisely the way the sculptor intended me to read it: as the promise of hope. The anarchists destroyed the baroque symbols of wealth inside Santa María, but the church still stands without the trappings of power. And Mary, that graceful personification of the dignity of the poor, poises on the verge of dancing. It has always saddened me that the anarchists felt they had to abandon her. Now I felt her buoying me.

And hope, after all, really does cost nothing. I returned from my trip to Catalonia to news of the American Catholic bishops organizing activists on behalf of undocumented immigrants, and felt humbled and instructed by their leadership. Not long after, I received a long hand-written letter from my mother. She is reading again, with a magnifying glass, and a new treatment has improved her eyesight significantly.

Gràcies a la Mare de Déu de l'Esperança.

Part Four

OTHER VOICES

~ 33 ~

Gratitude

John Garvey

In 1998 there was a book-burning in Ekaterinburg, Russia. An Orthodox bishop approved it. The books destroyed were by some of the leading Orthodox thinkers of our time: Alexander Schmemann, John Meyendorff, Nicholas Afanasiev, and Alexander Men. They were held to be contaminated by Western ideas, even heretical. The bishop was forced to resign, and the action was denounced, but the chill was felt throughout the Orthodox world. Add to this a number of other scandals, financial and sexual, involving priests, bishops, monks, and prominent laypeople, and it is enough to say that Roman Catholics need not feel alone: others have reasons to be discouraged with the church, if not reason to despair. The crises may be different, but they are there, and a few friends lose hope and drift away. If this is what the church comes down to — this fanaticism, or corruption, never dealt with for fear (ironically) of giving scandal, or because the organization is at heart an old-boy network — if this is all there is, why put up with it?

Once, when I was particularly discouraged, a good bishop told me, "Trees keep on growing, the Yankees keep on winning, and we are all still called to lives of holiness." This was before the Red Sox beat the Yankees, but he had a point. And yet the question of hope, of what hope means during bad times, matters deeply. More to the point, in what are we expected to place our hope?

There are understandable efforts to keep us from losing faith in the institution itself, and everyone has heard the basic argument: the church must have some sort of divine protection, because any other institution so thoroughly corrupt would have imploded long ago. By the time Paul wrote his first letter to the Corinthians (and we should remember that it was composed before any of the Gospels were written) the church was already a mess. If you take seriously the idea that the buying and selling of ecclesiastical offices renders them invalid, and if you also hold a more or less magical view of the apostolic succession (one still widely held), you have to conclude that true apostolic succession ended around the time Constantine made the church legal.

During a decadent time in the life of Russian Orthodoxy, St. Seraphim of Sarov lived a life that has been compared with that of Francis of Assisi, who also lived during one of the church's darkest times. It is right to look at such saints as signs that the word of God can be responded to at any point, and when this occurs, the response bears fruit, and this is a reason to hope.

But this isn't necessarily a reason to defend the institution. There is a certain smugness in the argument that although the church is corrupt, it is still around, so it must be doing something right. That's true as far as it goes, but we shouldn't let it go very far. If you take the incandescent love we see in Jesus Christ and in the lives of such saints as Seraphim and Francis, this sort of argument should shame us rather than console us in the twisted way it does. Having the effect of protecting the institution more than the message the institution was meant to be about, this emphasis can become not a reason for hope, but a recipe for cynicism, which is, if not quite despair, despair's handmaiden. The corruption of the church should be a cause for sorrow, but not a call to relax since things have often, maybe always, been this bad. And if you care for the institution at all, wounded and corrupt as it may be, you should worry at this point in history, when it is probably weaker than it has ever been. After the recent sexual scandals, church attendance in Ireland — perhaps the most Catholic country in Europe, with the possible exception of Poland — fell off drastically, not only among the young but among those over fifty. Church attendance in nominally Catholic and Orthodox countries (France, Italy, Greece, Romania) is very low. Combining this general indifference with smugness is a recipe for slow death, if that isn't what is already happening.

Weaker now than in the days of its beginning or during the persecution of early Christians by the Emperor Decius? Yes. Because Christianity was a fresh idea then. Now Christianity has a history — of great saints, true, and the first hospitals, and care for the poor — and pogroms, the Inquisition, anti-Semitism, a tolerance and even an occasional defense of slavery, the Thirty Years War, and hostility to what most Christians would now regard as fundamental liberties. It now comes across to many of our contemporaries as something old and dying, and they won't be sorry when it's dead.

Yet as Christians we are called to hope. Of the three great virtues, faith, hope, and charity, hope is the one that has most to do with the future, and it is entwined with faith. The Letter to the Hebrews says that faith "is the assurance of things hoped for, the conviction of things not seen." Hope is often falsely confused with a kind of optimism.

But the difference is that hope is expected to carry us through terrible times, even to the cross and beyond, while optimism assumes cheerily that the terrible times won't happen, or won't really be so terrible after all.

It is easy to see why the failures of the church tempt so many to lose hope. In many blighted lives the church — meaning the institution and its representatives — is the one place where people seek and sometimes find hope. When this church betrays you, when its representatives contradict what the church says it is about, you are tempted to give it up. This is true because for many people the church is an anesthetic, and its representatives carry more weight than perhaps they should, and among these people the damage caused by betrayal is greatest.

Marx is often misunderstood here — in his famous formulation, religion is "the opium of the people." But before this, he says, "Religion is the sigh of the oppressed creature, the heart of a heartless world." People who rely on the institution without looking beyond it are the most wounded when the church betrays them.

What must always be remembered is that even if the institutional church is necessary, as a kind of memory chain, a vehicle for transmission, it is not finally the real point, the object of our faith, our hope, or our love.

It seems to me that hopelessness is finally a kind of ingratitude — not for the institution, but toward God. If it were not for the presence of the corrupt institution in my own history I would not know anything about Jesus Christ and his presence in the sacraments, even if they have often been given to me by someone terribly flawed. In a wounded world both the priests and people who celebrate the sacraments are sleepwalkers, trying to awaken, and in the process stumbling, worshiping false gods (sex, money, power, prestige, security) along the way. These flawed people struggle to wake up, and a few do: saints, and some who are not saints but who burn with and for the Word and know that nothing else really matters. I think of someone as complicated as Simone Weil:

"Even if there were nothing more for us than life on earth, even if the instant of death were to bring us nothing new, the infinite superabundance of the divine mercy is already secretly present here below in its entirety.

"If, by an absurd hypothesis, I were to die without ever having committed any serious faults and yet all the same I were to fall to the bottom of hell, I should nevertheless owe God an infinite debt of gratitude for his infinite mercy, on account of my earthly life, and that notwithstanding the fact that I am such a poor unsatisfactory creature. Even in this hypothesis I should think all the same that I had received all my share of the riches of the divine mercy. For already here below we receive the capacity for loving God and for representing him to ourselves with complete certainty as having the substance of real, eternal, perfect, and infinite joy" (*Waiting for God,* Harper, 1973).

This reminds me of the words of an Orthodox saint, Silouan of Mount Athos (d. 1938), who in prayer was given this instruction: "Keep your mind in hell, and despair not."

I wish I could share Weil's complete certainty. I don't, and I am not sure that a certainty is called for in accepting her basic point, which has nothing to do with the church as an institution. Weil was writing about Christianity, which is more than bishops and parish priests.

We have to look to something deeper: It is possible to experience moments of sheer gratitude for the mere fact of consciousness, which fill you with gratitude for simply being — real moments of joy — and when you have known such moments you can begin to understand something of what she might mean. It helps also to meet people whose lives have been so informed by the gospel that they radiate its meaning. In both encounters — with moments in which the world shines with a presence that can't be put into words, and with holy people — is the ground of everything we need for hope.

The poet Robert Fitzgerald describes something wonderful and, I think, not all that uncommon. As a very young man he was taking a walk he took frequently, when "one afternoon I suffered, very suddenly, an entirely new sense of everything. I found myself unfamiliar. Nothing that I saw in this condition seemed familiar. Dimensions were felt to be arbitrary and precarious: the many trees, near and far, looked both like trees and like bunches of twigs fixed in the ground. It was as though the world had been made, or remade, in that instant: space, light, surfaces, bodies, all breathless with coming-to-be. Everything had become pure spectacle, subject to an unformulated but dazzling question: why all this, instead of nothing at all?" ("That Starry Country," in *The Third Kind of Knowledge,* New Directions, 1993).

I know a couple of things that I hope will carry me from now until the time of my death. I have learned about Jesus Christ from a group of people that includes saints and duplicitous scoundrels, but what I have learned gave me a hope that is in some way grounded in the sort of experience Fitzgerald describes, an experience that calls forth a profound gratitude. In some ways I feel like a kind of Christian agnostic. I know that I could be wrong. It could be, as Weil says, that death will end it — and even then I will be grateful for a few minutes of illuminated consciousness. That would have been enough. But I don't think that is all there is to it. When I am told by people who deny the existence of a deeper meaning, an eternal meaning, one that means resurrection into joy and eternal life, "What you have experienced there (in liturgy, in prayer, in reading the Gospels) is false, what you hope for isn't really what you think it is," I feel like someone who has read a wonderful poem, say one by Rilke, or has seen a glorious moment at the end of the day when the sun sets over Long Island Sound, and is told, "You may think that this is really beautiful, but it isn't"; or "What you really find good there doesn't have anything to do with the joy you think you feel." This doesn't square with my experience. And while my experience is far from anything like proof, I don't need proof, and don't think I am the kind of person for whom something like a logical proof would be convincing. It makes sense to me to try to live as if my experience of illumination were true, which means to live in hope.

✑ 34 ✑

Zion

Ruth Langer

The national anthem of the modern state of Israel is called "Hatiqvah," or "The Hope," and was adapted from "Our Hope," a somber Hebrew poem written in 1878 by Naphtali Herz Imber. This itinerant Galician poet, when visiting Palestine in 1882, shared his yet-unpublished poem with farmers in Rishon Lezion, a pioneer agricultural village founded the same year, one of whom set it to a European folk song (a theme also used by Smetana in his symphonic poem "The Moldau"). In Basel, in 1905, when the Sixth Zionist Congress concluded with everyone singing the song, Imber's poem became the unofficial anthem of the Zionist movement, a status that was made official in 1933. It served as the unofficial anthem of Jewish Palestine under the British Mandate, and, from the founding of the state of Israel in 1948, functioned as the nation's anthem. This status was officially confirmed in 2004.

Imber's original poem was a text of exile, reflecting the dominant religious expression of Jewish hope of the previous eighteen hundred years. This hope is messianic, explicitly grounded in God's promises transmitted by the biblical prophets, and elaborated upon by rabbinic traditions. It arises from the simple fact that without Jewish communal life in the Land of Israel, God's commandments in the Torah about agriculture, Temple worship, and self-government cannot be fulfilled. The rabbis established daily prayers that petition God for this promised messianic restoration, reminding the worshipers that even in the depths of exile, they had reasons to hope.

Imber's first stanza and the poem's refrain — which together became the anthem — express the Jews' yearning for a return to their homeland, reading:

> As long as in the innermost heart the Jewish soul
>   is longing,
> And towards the east, its eye is searching for Zion —
> Then our hope has not been lost, the ancient hope
> To return to the land of our ancestors, to the city
>   where David camped.

The following stanzas develop this theme, all but the last beginning "as long as" and describing some basis for the persistence of Jewish hope. These range from the relatively benign flow of the Jordan River into the Sea of Galilee, to descriptions of and allusions to Jewish tears and mourning practices over the destruction of Jerusalem and its Temple, to the practically miraculous fact that Jews have survived this exile. The final verse states that the Jewish hope can never end as long as there are Jews alive.

Informing the poem's tone and much of its language are traditions of Jewish poetic elaborations on the biblical book of Lamentations, recited annually on the anniversary of the destructions of the Jerusalem Temples in 586 B.C.E. and 70 C.E.; and leavening that mourning was hope. This hope, about which Imber writes, is *the* hope that sustained Jews during the troubled centuries of exile: the belief that although God had imposed these punishments on the people Israel in angry response to their transgressions, God has also promised a messianic reversal of this ill-fortune.

The critical elements of this messianic reversal include, first and foremost, a restoration of Jewish national life in the land of Israel, with Jerusalem, also called Zion after one of its hills, at its heart. Imber's reference to Jerusalem as the place where "David camped" alludes to other aspects of this scenario: the restoration of Davidic sovereignty over this nation-state in the person of his descendent, the anointed king, the Messiah; and the rebuilding of the Jerusalem Temple on the site to which the biblical King David had brought the ark of the covenant after his conquest of Jerusalem and his decisive defeat of the Philistines. God permitted David, the warrior king, to erect only a tent for it there, leaving the building of the Temple proper to his son, King Solomon.

This summoning of eschatological hope in the midst of the misery of exile was characteristic of Jewish theology, expressed in popular religiosity as well as in learned literature, until modernity and the birth in the late nineteenth century of the Zionist movement. Zionism — as it became known — was in many of its forms an activist and nationalist adaptation of traditional messianism. Always in its secular manifestations and frequently in its religious expressions too, Zionism rejected Judaism's traditional patient acceptance of exile and suffering and called instead for active efforts to *realize* at least elements of this ancient hope for redemption. The Holocaust reinforced this; it was apparent to Jews that they could no longer afford to be history's passive victims while awaiting divine intervention; rather they would work to shape history themselves.

◆ ◆ ◆

Over the course of the years, the Zionist anthem penned by Imber underwent multiple revisions. Today the official anthem of the State of Israel contains, as noted above, only Imber's first stanza and the refrain, though the refrain is almost unrecognizable. It now reads:

Then our hope has not yet been lost, the hope of
    two thousand years
To be a free people in our land, the land of Israel
    and Jerusalem.

The changes to the first line are mostly a matter of developing a rhyme to go with the radically transformed second line, which now suggests that Jews residing in the land of Israel have fulfilled the hope of a return to Zion. Additionally, the refrain deliberately no longer refers to the Temple. In fact, shortening the anthem to a single stanza excised Imber's references to most elements of a messianic restoration as well as to the mourning typical of the exilic state of mind. The modern anthem, then, presents a revised expression of hope, one that relies on people and not on God, and one that expects the fruits of the traditional messianic redemption — the prophetic visions of peace and prosperity for all humanity — without restorations of the Davidic monarchy or sacrificial worship in Jerusalem. There is no Messiah and no resurrection of the dead (something Imber had obliquely alluded to). There is only an ingathering of the exiles.

Modernized eschatological visions were not the invention of Zionism. Nineteenth-century Reform Judaism, particularly in Germany and America, had called for elimination of the supernatural elements of Jewish messianism and expressed their hope for the manifestation of a "Messianic Age," a utopia that would include all humanity. They rejected any dreams of the establishment of a Jewish state in Zion as incompatible with the newfound status of Jews as citizens in the Western world. Jewish particularism countered God's will, they opined, while scattered Jews witnessed to God more effectively. Secular Zionists rejected the reformer's vision. A century of emancipation with continuing anti-Semitism in the West, and the resumption of deadly anti-Jewish pogroms in Eastern Europe, had taught them that Jews could live normal lives only in their own homeland. Their eyes were "towards the east, . . . searching for Zion."

Hope, then, for Jews, is literally found on the ground, on this earth. For Jews across political and religious spectrums, hope consists of an understanding that our world is not in its perfect state, combined with a confidence that the world is also ultimately perfectible. Jews differ on the degree of divine intervention necessary in this process, but generally agree that human efforts also play a role, whether through prayer and mystical meditation or through concrete, practical actions. As Imber's poem and Israel's national anthem state, this ancient hope is what sustained and sustains Jews in times of trouble. As Israel today again faces enemies sworn to destroy her, this hope to live in a world of justice, prosperity, and peace, "to be a free people in our land," gives continuing meaning to her struggles.

~ 35 ~

Recovery Movement
Martin E. Marty

The first step in recovering hope is to separate it radically from optimism, with which it is so often confused. When confronted by someone who would confuse the two, I recite a little poem, "The Optimist":

> The optimist fell ten stories,
> As he passed each window bar
> He shouted in to his comrades,
> "It's all right so far!"

Such an optimist is destined to make a quick splash, and what he has done and asserted has nothing to do with any version of hope. Admittedly, he could hope that the fire department happens to be on hand with a net, but he is in these lines too busy shouting to be able to calculate details of his imminent landing.

The second step in recovering hope is to describe the context for hope in time and space. My colleague

213

Fr. David Tracy taught me three words that I have so internalized that they form a rubric. Before one expresses faith or love — or hope! — he or she must consider "finitude, contingency, and transience." Out of such awareness comes the realism that Christians associate, or ought to associate, with hope.

Finitude: you will die. You might hope that you will live, and Christians believe that love is stronger than death, so death is not the last word. But death denies one kind of hope.

Contingency: the optimist happened to fall out of the ten-story window. Accidents happen. One may hope that contingency, in the form of good luck, will also be in effect, but coins come up tails as often as heads, and most lottery players, who hope they will win, cannot. Christian hope has to transcend the contingencies of life in the world.

Transience: we read of fools who hope to be remembered because they have built monuments to, or mausoleums for, themselves; they are buying into short-term delusion. Everything changes, and everything belonging to this earth passes. Hope directed against transience is futile.

The third step in clearing the way for the recovery of hope is to note where it reposes: within the person. In this regard, the most helpful humanistic words of our time were expressed by the psychiatrist and death camp inmate Viktor Frankl, who testified, in *Man's Search for*

Meaning, to observing other inmates who knew they were soon to be killed but who nonetheless "walked through the huts comforting others, giving away their last piece of bread." He went on: "Everything can be taken from a man but one thing, the last of the human freedoms — to choose one's attitude in any given set of circumstances — to choose one's own way." In another place Frankl wrote that these individuals demonstrated "the fact that the last inner freedom cannot be lost." We are fortunate that Frankl survived. Had he been killed, we would not have his words, though someone with Frankl's philosophy had to believe in the intrinsic value of hope, irrespective of hoping's outcomes.

Rereading Frankl, as I often have, however, leads me to add, with respect, a Christian refinement. His words stress *"a* person" ("man"), *"one's"* attitude, and choosing *"one's"* way, as if in isolation. Testifying as a Christian, however — and based on my baptism and life in eucharistic community — I would say that hope is "inner" to the person *and* the communion. This means to me that whenever the sign of the cross is made on the forehead of an infant being baptized or that of the comatose dying senior, the community of hope is in that person's company, witnessing to a hope not limited by finitude, contingency, and transience.

So it is that at the Eucharist, in our part of the Christian church, we sing about this meal as a "foretaste of the feast to come." If Christians believe in what Jesus says in

215

Luke's Gospel (22:14), they will find hope here shading into the concept of desire: "I have eagerly desired to eat this Passover with you before I suffer, for I tell you, I will not eat it until it is fulfilled in the kingdom of God." Explicit "hope" turns up later in the most pathetic line in that Gospel, wherein on the evening of the resurrection two followers on the road to Emmaus were confronted by an inquiring stranger. To him they said — note the past perfect tense — "We *had* hoped that [Jesus of Nazareth] was the one to redeem Israel" (Luke 24:21). Hope was renewed a few hours and a few lines later when, at an inn, he "took bread, blessed and broke it, and gave it to them . . . and they recognized him" (Luke 28:30–31).

In my own life, having seen numberless hopes dashed and forgotten, I call to mind the times when my ability to draw on the "inner freedom" of individual and communal life meant most to me. These were at the deathbeds of both parents and of my first wife, and in the presence of parishioners on whom I called at dying time during ten years of pastorate. Under these circumstances, when we might be properly outraged when told by well-wishers that we should "hope for a miracle," we are encouraged nonetheless to hope and to locate our hopes in a "set of circumstances" beyond what is finite, contingent, and transient.

Realistic hope, however, also needs to be available to us this side of death camps and deathbeds, for most of life is ordinary, quotidian, served up into almost manageable segments called "days." Disappointment (so far) would not be featured prominently in my own memoir; enough things have gone sufficiently well. My calling as a teacher, however, takes me into the circle of generations of students who did not win the hoped-for fellowship or prize or grade "A" or, more drastically, the tenureable position for which they were well prepared (their teacher thought and insisted).

Here is where counsel, empathy, and vision become important. In preparation for encounters with the fruitless job-seeker and others in similar circumstances, I turn to another biblical text, this written by Paul the Apostle to people in circumstances more dire than I have just described. I should try to climax this little essay with some words of my own, but I realistically hope that it will mean more to readers simply to take these words from Romans 5:5: ... *knowing that suffering produces endurance, and endurance produces character, and character produces hope, and hope does not disappoint us.*

Contributors

Msgr. Lorenzo Albacete is the U.S. director of the Fraternity of Communion and Liberation, an international ecclesial movement, and is the author of *God at the Ritz: Attraction to Infinity* (Crossroad, 2002).

Ben Birnbaum is the editor of *Boston College Magazine* as well as special assistant to the president and executive director of the Office of Marketing Communications at Boston College. His work has been anthologized in *Best American Essays, Best Spiritual Writing,* and *Best Catholic Writing.*

Lisa Sowle Cahill is the J. Donald Monan Professor of Theology at Boston College. She works in the area of Christian social ethics, including gender and family ethics, war and peace, and bioethics. Her most recent book is *Theological Bioethics: Participation, Justice and Change* (Georgetown, 2005).

Colleen Carroll Campbell, a fellow at the Ethics and Public Policy Center, is a columnist, television host, former speechwriter for President George W. Bush, and author of *The New Faithful: Why Young Adults Are Embracing Christian Orthodoxy* (Loyola, 2002).

Lawrence S. Cunningham is the John A. O'Brien Professor of Theology at the University of Notre Dame. His most recent book is *A Brief History of the Saints* (Blackwell, 2004).

Brian Doyle is the editor of *Portland Magazine* at the University of Portland, in Oregon. He is the author of eight books, including *The Wet Engine* (Paraclete, 2005), about hearts, *The Grail* (Oregon State University, 2006), about wine, and, most recently, *Epiphanies & Elegies,* a collection of poems.

Paul Elie is the author of *The Life You Save May Be Your Own: An American Pilgrimage* (Farrar, Straus & Giroux, 2003). His article "The Year of Two Popes" appeared in the January–February 2006 *Atlantic Monthly.*

Harold Fickett is the author of *The Holy Fool* (Crossway, 1983), *The Living Christ* (Doubleday, 2002), and many other books. He is a contributing editor to the online magazine *GodSpy* (*www.godspy.com*).

John Garvey is a priest of the Orthodox Church in America and a columnist for *Commonweal.* His most recent books are *Seeds of the Word: Orthodox Thinking on Other Religions* (St. Vladimir's Seminary Press, 2005) and *Death and the Rest of Our Life* (Eerdmans, 2005).

Paul J. Griffiths holds the Schmitt Chair in Catholic Studies at the University of Illinois at Chicago and, beginning in January 2008, will hold the Warren Chair of Catholic Thought at Duke Divinity School. He is the author or co-author of thirteen books including *Reason and the Reasons of Faith,* co-edited with Reinhard Hütter (T. & T. Clark, 2005), *Lying: An Augustinian Theology of Duplicity* (Brazos, 2004), and *Problems of Religious Diversity* (Blackwell, 2001). He is currently working on three books: *The Vice of Curiosity: An Essay on the Nature of Intellectual Appetite;* a Christian commentary on the *Vijñaptimatratasiddhi;* and *How Catholics Think: An Essay on Intellectual Style.*

A. G. Harmon's essays and fiction have appeared in numerous publications. His novel *A House All Stilled* (University of Tennessee, 2002) was awarded the Peter Taylor Prize for the Novel in 2001. He teaches at the Catholic University of America in Washington, D.C.

Jeanine Hathaway is the author of the autobiographical novel *Motherhouse* (Hyperion, 1992) and a collection of poems, *The Self as Constellation* (University of North Texas Press, 2002). She teaches at Wichita State University.

Fr. Michael Heher is the Vicar General and Moderator of the Curia of the Diocese of Orange. He is the author of *The Lost Art of Walking on Water: Reimagining the Priesthood* (Paulist Press, 2004). He holds a doctorate in theology from the Pontifical Gregorian University in Rome.

221

Paula Huston, a Camaldolese Benedictine oblate, is the author of four books, along with a number of short stories and essays. Her most recent project, *By Way of Grace: Moving from Faithfulness to Holiness* (Loyola Press, 2007), looks at the cardinal and theological virtues in light of Christian transformation.

Robert Imbelli is a priest of the Archdiocese of New York and associate professor of theology at Boston College. An abiding concern is the inseparability of theology and spirituality and poetry's power to evoke the wonder of a world "charged with the glory of God."

Luke Timothy Johnson is Robert W. Woodruff Professor of New Testament and Christian Origins in the Candler School of Theology at Emory University. He is the author of twenty-five books, including *Reading Romans: A Literary and Theological Commentary* (Smyth & Helwys, 1999); and *Living Jesus: Learning the Heart of the Gospels* (HarperSanFrancisco, 1999).

Peter Kreeft is a professor of philosophy at Boston College, where he has worked since 1965. He is the author of forty-eight books.

Ruth Langer is a rabbi, a member of the theology faculty at Boston College, and associate director of the university's Center for Christian-Jewish Learning. The author of *To Worship God Properly* (Hebrew Union College, 1998), she writes about the history of Jewish liturgy and ritual and on Christian-Jewish relations.

Paul Mariani is an award-winning poet and the author of fifteen books, including biographies of William Carlos Williams, Robert Lowell, and Hart Crane. He teaches at Boston College as the University Professor of English and is at work on a biography of Gerard Manley Hopkins.

James Martin is a Jesuit priest and associate editor of *America* magazine. He is the author or editor of seven books, including a memoir entitled *My Life with the Saints* (Loyola Press, 2006).

Martin E. Marty is the Fairfax M. Cone Distinguished Service Professor Emeritus at the University of Chicago. He is the author or editor of more than fifty books, including, most recently, *The Mystery of the Child* (Eerdmans, 2007).

Cullen Murphy is the editor at large of *Vanity Fair* and was for twenty years the managing editor of the *Atlantic Monthly*. His most recent book is *Are We Rome? The Fall of an Empire and the Fate of America* (Houghton Mifflin, 2007).

Melissa Musick Nussbaum is the author of five books and numerous articles on liturgy and faith formation. She is a columnist for *Celebration* and *GIA Quarterly*. She and her husband are the parents of five children and the grandparents of three.

Joseph Pearce is writer-in-residence and associate professor of literature at Ave Maria University in Naples, Florida. He is co-editor of the *Saint Austin Review* and author of many books, including biographies of Tolkien, C. S. Lewis, Chesterton, Solzhenitsyn, and Oscar Wilde.

Timothy Radcliffe, O.P., taught at Blackfriars, Oxford, for many years. He was Master of the Dominican Order and won the Michael Ramsey Prize for Theological Writing 2006/7.

Peggy Rosenthal is the author of *The Poets' Jesus: Representations at the End of a Millennium* and co-editor of *Divine Inspiration: The Life of Jesus in World Poetry* (both Oxford University Press). She is also the author of the reflection guides *Praying the Gospels through Poetry* and *Praying through Poetry: Hope for Violent Times* (both St. Anthony Messenger Press).

Robert Royal is president of the Faith & Reason Institute in Washington, D.C. His most recent book is *The God That Did Not Fail: How Religion Built and Sustains the West* (Encounter, 2006).

Valerie Sayers is the author of five novels and a professor of English at the University of Notre Dame. She has received a National Endowment for the Arts literature fellowship and a Pushcart Prize, and her stories, essays, and reviews appear widely.

Richard K. Taylor is a parishioner and a staff member of St. Vincent de Paul Church in Philadelphia, and he has served on the Archdiocese of Philadelphia's Commission on World Peace and Justice. He is the author of *Love in Action: A Direct Action Handbook for Catholics Using Gospel Non-Violence to Reform and Renew the Church.*

Paul Wilkes is the author of eighteen nonfiction books and a novel, a producer of PBS documentaries, and the creator of New Beginnings (*nbontheweb.com*), which fosters parish vitality and stewardship. Among his books are *Best Practices from America's Best Churches* (Paulist, 2003), and *Beyond the Walls: Monastic Wisdom for Everyday Life* (Doubleday, 1999).

Gregory Wolfe is the editor of *Image* and serves as director of the Master of Fine Arts in Creative Writing program at Seattle Pacific University. His website is *www.gregorywolfe.com.*

Kenneth L. Woodward was for thirty-eight years Religion Editor of *Newsweek* and is the author of three books. He is writing a memoir of American religion from the Age of Eisenhower to the Era of George W. Bush.

Ann Wroe is the special reports and obituaries editor of *The Economist* and the author of *Pontius Pilate* (Random House, 2000). Her latest book, published by Pantheon in 2007, is *Being Shelley: The Poet's Search for Himself,* a metaphysical biography of Percy Bysshe Shelley.

Contributors

Don Wycliff was a newspaper journalist for thirty-five years, including five as a member of the *New York Times* editorial board and nine as editorial page editor of the *Chicago Tribune.* He is an administrator and teacher of journalism at the University of Notre Dame.

Phyllis Zagano is senior research associate-in-residence at Hofstra University, a Catholic columnist for Religion News Service, and author of several books in Catholic Studies, including *Holy Saturday: An Argument for the Restoration of the Female Diaconate in the Catholic Church* (Herder & Herder, 2000).

Philip Zaleski is the coauthor of *Prayer: A History* (Houghton Mifflin, 2005) and the editor of the *Best American Spiritual Writing* series.

Index

227

Index

Of Related Interest

Lorenzo Albacete
GOD AT THE RITZ
Attraction to Infinity

"Lorenzo Albacete is one of a kind, and so is *God at the Ritz*. The book, like the monsignor, crackles with humor, warmth, and intellectual excitement. Reading it is like having a stay-up-all-night, jump-out-of-your-chair, have-another-double-espresso marathon conversation with one of the world's most swashbuckling talkers. Conversation, heck — this is a papal bull session!"

— Hendrik Hertzberg, *The New Yorker Magazine*

0-8245-2472-1, paperback

Check your local bookstore for availability.
To order directly from the publisher,
please call 1-800-707-0670 for Customer Service
or visit our Web site at *www.cpcbooks.com.*
For catalog orders, please send your request to the address below.

THE CROSSROAD PUBLISHING COMPANY
16 Penn Plaza, Suite 1550
New York, NY 10001

crossroad